JUDGED BY THE LAW OF FREEDOM

A History of the Faith-Works Controversy, and a Resolution in the Thought of St. Thomas Aquinas

Richard H. Bulzacchelli

University Press of America,® Inc.
Lanham · Boulder · New York · Toronto · Oxford

Copyright © 2006 by
University Press of America,® Inc.
4501 Forbes Boulevard
Suite 200
Lanham, Maryland 20706
UPA Acquisitions Department (301) 459-3366

PO Box 317
Oxford
OX2 9RU, UK

All rights reserved
Printed in the United States of America
British Library Cataloging in Publication Information Available

Library of Congress Control Number: 2006923922
ISBN-13: 978-0-7618-3501-1 (paperback : alk. paper)

∞™ The paper used in this publication meets the minimum
requirements of American National Standard for Information
Sciences—Permanence of Paper for Printed Library Materials,
ANSI Z39.48—1984

Dedication

To St. Thomas Aquinas, who taught me how to distinguish; and to my wife, Kay, who has been patient with me. Along with my own effort in grace, I offer their prayers and sacrifices as they pertain to this project, for the unity of the Church, and the good of souls, if Christ so wills.

Contents

Preface · vii
Acknowledgments · ix
Introduction · xi

Part I
The Paradox of Faith and Works:
Reconciling Divine Causality with Human Free-Will and Merit

Chapter 1: Stating the Problem: Human Achievement or Divine Causality? · 3

Chapter 2: A History of the Faith-Works Controversy · 11
  The Apostolic Age: Legalism vs. Gnosticism in the New Testament · 12
  The Controversy between Augustine and Pelagianism · 25
  The Reformation: Calvinism, Lutheranism, and the Council of Trent · 35
  The *de Auxiliis* Controversy and its Aftermath · 40

Part II
A Resolution of this Paradox in the Thought of St. Thomas Aquinas

Chapter 3: Aquinas on Causality in Nature and Grace · 51
  Distinguishing between Aristotle and Aquinas on the Four Causes · 51
  God as Final and Efficient Cause of the Human Being · 61
  God as Quasi-Formal Cause of the Will in Charity · 78

Chapter 4: Aquinas on Merit in Nature and Grace · 81
  The Question of Perseverance: Suggestions for a Different Approach · 89

Concluding Remarks: The Present Study and the Challenge of Ecumenical Dialogue in a Post-Modern Society · 101

Bibliography: · 111

About the Author: · 117

Preface

The present study began as a paper submitted to Rev. Lawrence Donohoo, O.P., for a course in moral theology at the Dominican House of Studies in Washington, DC. After considerable development, that paper evolved into my S.T.L. dissertation, directed by Rev. Norman Fenton, O.P. Fr. Fenton encouraged me to go further with the work, and to publish it, when ready, as a monograph. Here, in the present volume, you have the product of that effort. Portions of this work have been excised, while others have been developed more fully. The work has been restructured, and, in places, rephrased. It remains, however, at the end of this process, as it was: a *hybrid*. That fact may appeal to some, while others may judge it to be a weakness. It has seemed to me, however, that a *hybrid* work is precisely what the present study required, were it to achieve its intended purpose. I meant to provide a reading of Aquinas' treatment of the faith-works paradox from a fresh perspective, while providing the historical context within which the reader can see precisely why it is important to affirm that paradox intact, and to find the metaphysical language with which to articulate it coherently.

On the one hand, therefore, there is something for the generalist in this volume. In the first part of the book, I treat a broad history of controversy, but without undue attention to purely historical detail. I offer, rather, a history of *ideas*, drawn out for the reader in broad lines of thought, illustrating *trajectories*. I make no pretense, here, of having offered an exhaustive treatment. Instead, the interested reader should understand that my subject is not so much Augustine, or Cassian, or Calvin, or Luther, or Báñez, or Molina; it is, rather, a *paradox* as it makes itself known and felt in the minds and the hearts of Christian thinkers in all times. It is the paradox of saying that while human beings are, in some sense, *responsible* for whether or not we are saved, we are, nonetheless, radically and inescapably *dependent upon God* for everything we are and do, especially in the order of salvation.

On the other hand, there is something in this book for the specialist. A serious student of St. Thomas Aquinas, or of Mediaeval philosophy and theology, will find, in Part II of this book, a careful synthesis of a broad selection of texts from the Angelic Doctor. I treat Aquinas as a *hylomorphist* with his own particular take on what that metaphysic entails, especially with respect to the paradox at hand. I present, to the reader, my own translations of Aquinas' words, and the Latin from which these translations are made, because, I suggest, the main thrust of his argument, or the point he is attempting to make by it, often hinges upon the subtle nuances of a particular word or phrase.

In the end, however, if there is, as I hope, something worthwhile in this book for the reader, that reader should note that the book in question is offered, first of all, in the service of the Church. As a theologian, I understand my scholarly efforts always with reference to *her*—to the Church, who is the "Bride of Christ". It is for her to scrutinize, to critique, and to correct; and if God has blessed me with any real insight into the meaning of divine revelation, my work is for the Church to use, as she leads more souls, my own among them, to heaven. I offer the present volume, therefore, with the assent of intellect and will to the constant teaching and Tradition of the Church on matters of faith and morals, and in submission to the judgment of her Magisterium in communion with the Successor of St. Peter.

RICHARD H. BULZACCHELLI

Aquinas College
Nashville, Tennessee

Feast of the Triumph of the Cross
September 14, 2005

Acknowledgements

After a good deal of proof-reading and revision, it is for me to admit that any errors remaining in the present volume are my own responsibility. I have attempted, throughout, to be true to my sources, to be honest about the views of those with whom I take issue, and most of all, to accurately represent the Scriptures as interpreted by the Church in her teaching and Tradition. If, in my human fallibility, I have fallen short by any of these measures, the reader is asked to accept that this failing, while my own, runs contrary to my true intentions.

As I bring this book to completion, of course, I wish to thank, most of all, my wife, Kay. She has shared my life with me for several years now, and has, therefore, in a real sense, spent nearly as much time with this book as I have. Rev. Norman Fenton, O.P., and Rev. Thomas Acklin, O.S.B., who read this manuscript at a much earlier stage of its development, and offered me their constructive comments and their encouragement, deserve to be recognized as well. My colleague, Peter A. Pagan Aguiar, Ph.D., merits no less thanks. Through an ongoing *disputatio* with him on matters pertaining to the present thesis, I have come to further clarify my own thinking, and to see with greater accuracy where my considerations, and those of Aquinas, begin to diverge. I must, further, recognize the efforts of my long-time friend, Kristine F. Keller, who helped prepare the final manuscript.

I owe an inexhaustible debt, of course, to the venerable scholars of the Leonine Commission. For over a century, their task has been to study the texts of Aquinas so as to provide reliable manuscripts of his works, and from these, to develop, for the scholarly community, critical editions of those manuscripts. I have taken my Latin texts of Aquinas' works largely from what they have contributed. For the *Summa Theologiae*, I have employed the reliable and widely accessible Marietti edition.

Acknowledgment is also due to the Anglican divines of the late nineteenth century. While they may have made many editorial judgments with which I do not agree, they did the Christian world an overall service in supplying English translations of so many of the Fathers of the Church. Relevant to the present volume are their two series of, *The Nicene and Post-Nicene Fathers of the Christian Church*.

Direct quotations from Scripture in this text are excerpts from the *New American Bible with Revised New Testament* Copyright © 1986, 1970 Confraternity of Christian Doctrine, Inc., Washington, DC. Used with permission. All rights reserved. No portion of the *New American Bible* may be reprinted without permission in writing from the copyright holder.

Introduction

Among the central paradoxes of orthodox Christianity we find the claim that, on the one hand, human beings are radically dependent upon God for our salvation, while on the other hand, we are somehow responsible for whether or not we are saved. On the one hand, that is, what we do, morally, makes a difference in our spiritual condition; on the other hand, our spiritual condition is utterly contingent upon whether God grants or withholds his grace from us. The attempt within Christianity to maintain both these truths simultaneously has been a focal point of serious and recurrent tensions over the Church's two-thousand year history. The emphasis upon one component of the orthodox position at the exclusion of the other is a constant risk. When failure occurs at this point, a wide variety of heresies arise, from Pelagianism on the one hand, to radical Predestinarianism on the other, and from the trivialization of, on the one hand, *God*, and on the other, *humanity*.

Central to this paradox is the question of *theological virtue*—that is to say, those special virtues initially acquired, not through natural habituation and practice, but through *divine causality* exercising a direct infusion of grace. We must, therefore, examine the relationship between God's causal agency in supplying *theological virtue* to the human person, and (if any) the human person's own meritorious agency. We need not dwell, at length, upon any hard and fast distinction between the various theological virtues, entering into a separate analysis of each virtue, one-by-one. This is because we are here concerned principally, not with this or that *particular* theological virtue, but with their *causes*. Thus, when we speak, in this work, about *causality in theological virtue*, we are concerned with a discussion of the causal principles behind the complete *life of faith*. This involves the initial act of assent, as well as the *habitus* of faith, sustained over time, given the character of a pilgrimage in hope, and culminating in charity, its full form. When we speak, in this work, then, of the *assent into faith*, we mean more than just the initial act of assent at the moment one wills to believe, but the movement of the human person into the life of faith as we have just described it.[1]

We focus, in this study, then, upon the relationship between God's causality at work in theological virtue in human beings and the prospect of human "meriting"[2] of the rewards of salvation. Christians have always held that salvation and faith are *truly interrelated*; but the *nature* of that relationship has been debated perpetually. We consider this paradox in the present volume, with an eye toward, at last, suggesting a coherent resolution built upon a foundation of both metaphysical and scriptural integrity.

We divide our study, therefore, into two major parts, numbering our chapters continuously throughout.[3] With Part I, we provide the reader with a broad sense of the history of this paradox as it has arisen throughout the life of the Church, and of the root metaphysical and theological issues at the heart of the resulting conflicts. With Part II of our study, we propose a resolution of the paradox at hand, grounded in the thought of St. Thomas Aquinas.

Part I comprises two chapters of the book. In the first chapter of Part I, we consider the respective theses of the two extremes of the paradox at hand: Predestinarianism on the one hand, and Pelagianism on the other. We ask in each case, what, precisely is at issue, both for the adherent and the opponent of the position in question. With the second chapter of Part I, we provide a brief sketch of the history of this conflict

---

1. Our subject, then, is the (in the end, primarily Thomistic) metaphysical analysis of what St. Bonaventure treats contemplatively in his *Itinerarium Mentis in Deum*. Thus, we are here concerned not only with an *assent* to a proposition, but also, and indeed, more fundamentally, with an *ascent* of the human person to a higher life.

2. "Meriting" appears here in quotation marks to remind the reader that the term is being applied analogously. That is not to suggest the denial of any *real* merit; it is only to say that, when speaking of merit before *God*, we are not using the term *merit* in quite the same sense in which we use it when speaking, for example, of merit before another human being. We *must* remember this if we are to fully understand Aquinas' position.

3. The fist chapter of Part II is Chapter 3.

throughout the Church's life. Our sketch begins with the early Church, and continues through the Patristic and Medieval periods, and forward to the Reformation and Tridentine periods. This survey, as we have suggested, is intentionally concise, since its function for us here is *not* one of *evidence* but one of *context*. While we attempt to treat with fairness those figures under consideration in this section of our study, we remain aware of the limits of the present project, and the fact that, at times, only light *sketches*, rather than detailed portraits, can be drawn. The material presented in Part I of this book, therefore, is intended to set the historical stage—to provide a kind of backdrop—for our much more detailed examination of the thought of St. Thomas Aquinas, on the basis of which we propose a resolution of the paradox in question.

Part II of our study is, thus, a discussion of Aquinas' treatment of the paradox presented in Part I. Part II is the central focus of our project, and as such, will consist of a more concentrated and detailed scholarly examination of the paradox at issue. This part of our study comprises two chapters of the book, and will be based upon a thorough investigation of the primary texts within Aquinas' own works. That is to say that we will not seek out any particular Thom-*ism*, as such, but will rest upon a direct analysis of Aquinas' own texts. This is, we suggest, important for the attainment of our goal. As illustrated in our treatment, in the present volume, of the *Congregatio de Auxiliis*, for example, major Thomistic interpretations of this question do not necessarily reflect the thought of Aquinas himself on this subject, nor do their respective approaches to the major components of the paradox always agree. Aquinas, for his own part, does not offer a systematic treatise on the precise subject under discussion here. His thought on this paradox must be woven together from a wholistic reading of his works. Disagreement, concerning this question, between disparate Thomistic schools, therefore, arose, historically, out of commentaries upon the treatises Aquinas did, in fact, write. In these, Commentators applied Thomistic metaphysical categories to the paradox at hand, from within the limited framework of Aquinas' discussion of *foreknowledge* or *eternity*, or *predestination*, or *the Book of Life*. They did not, however, go further, asking whether other categories might yield better fruit when applied to an understanding of the issue at hand, or whether other lines of thought, or other emphases, might shed clearer light, casting the issue in language better suited to communicate the Scriptural revelation of a profoundly personal God of overflowing mercy and compassion. We intend, therefore, to start fresh with this paradox in the thought of St. Thomas Aquinas, turning to his texts as a whole, rather than limiting our consideration to a particular treatise, into which the paradox must be fitted by force. In fact, in the interest of this endeavor, we deliberately attempt to avoid those old controversies.

In the first chapter of Part II (i.e., Chapter 3) of this book, therefore, we discuss Aquinas' treatment of *causality* in nature and in grace. We begin by framing *Aquinas'* understanding of causality in contradistinction to that of *Aristotle*, under the premise that Aquinas is frequently, and wrongly, reduced to Aristotle on this point, and *vice-versa*. We thus discuss points of distinction between Aquinas and Aristotle on the question of causality, based upon their differing convictions concerning the character of God and our relationship to him. We then turn, in earnest, to our analysis of Aquinas' texts central to the discussion of causality in nature and grace. Within this analysis we treat the question of God as *final* and *efficient* cause of human being, including a discussion of the causation by God of a *free-will* in human beings, both at the level of nature and at the level of grace. We also discuss the human being's causative act within the process of free-choice both within the context of nature and of grace. Our discussion proceeds through a treatment of God's final causation of human being in the infusion of theological virtue, to a treatment of so-called *quasi-formal* causality by God, of the human will in the theological virtue of charity.

The second chapter dealing with the analysis of Aquinas' position (i.e., Chapter 4) deals with his treatment of *merit* in nature and grace. There, we discuss the conditions for merit considered *simply* and *relatively*, out of *condignity* and out of *congruency*. We also consider the topic of human merit before God, in the various senses in which that can or cannot be claimed within the contexts of nature and of grace. We will see that, for Aquinas, the indwelling of the Holy Spirit is the cause of condignity between the human person and God; and the relevance of this thesis to the resolution we seek should then be made clear. It is for us to discuss, therefore, the analogous sense of condignity in this event given the fact of *quasi*, not *per se*, formal causality. We then consider, finally, the objects of human meriting in grace, namely, help for others (*Summa Theologiae* I-II.6), growth in one's own life of grace (ibid. I-II.8), and the rewards of salvation (ibid. I-II.8–9).

In Part II of this study, therefore, we present the thesis that for Aquinas, human beings are *dependent upon God* for their rise into a life of grace, and thus, for salvation, in that we do not have within our natural ontological limits the inherent power to will an object or to know an object which is ontologically greater than our will and our intellect. This means that human beings must be raised to an assent to the infinite *by* the infinite, i.e. by God. At the same time, our freedom is not negated by this elevation because God does not cause this elevation in a *forceful* or *coercive* way, but causes it by *ontologically under-girding* our free-choice and our intellect, *enabling* or *empowering* us to achieve by his assistance what would be otherwise impossible for us even to attempt. *Merit is possible* in this context, furthermore, because when the will comes to rest in the Holy Spirit and cleave to him, the Holy Spirit fulfills the will's ultimate *telos*, becoming for this will, a *quasi-form*. It is *as if* the Holy Spirit *is* the *will-in-form*, since it is the *end toward which* the will is directed by divine ordination, and *now realized*. Thus, when God looks upon a human being, he sees his equal, *himself*, there—a being which *can* merit before him. Yet this is *not* merely *forensic* justification,[4] since it is truly *my* will which is cleaving to this meritorious fulfillment. My will is *enabled* or *empowered* by

---

4. The phrase *forensic justification* refers to the view articulated by Luther, Calvin, and other Reformers, that human beings are never rendered *internally righteous* by God, but that we are simply *regarded* by God *as if* we are righteous. In other words, according to the claim of *forensic justification*, God *acts as if* we are righteous, even though, *in actual fact*, we are not. The Roman Catholic Church has always rejected this claim in favor of the position that Christ actually *restores* and even *elevates* human beings to a condition above our nature, so that we could, in fact, enter into a *relationship* with one who is above our nature—i.e. *God*. Many Protestants, however, observe that human beings continue to struggle with sin throughout life, and argue that if we were, in fact, internally conformed to the will of God, we would not face such a struggle. Catholics respond to this argument with the suggestion that because we are both spiritual *and* corporeal beings, there is a dimension of the human person and the human will, which awaits, for its full restoration, *the resurrection of the body and the life of the world to come*. Nonetheless, human beings are *internally* justified—that dimension of the human will that is *spiritual* is truly conformed to God, united to him in friendship, and indwelt by the Holy Spirit. Were it *otherwise*, God could not act *as if* it were so without denying the Truth; but this would be absurd, for God, from any orthodox point of view, can never deny the Truth. Indeed, this is as much a purely *philosophical* certainty as it is a certainty of the faith. See note 49.

God to do this, *elevated* by God to a supernatural condition, and *sustained* in that condition of agency by God's *agency-in-grace*. Precisely by virtue of *God's* causal activity of grace, however, it is truly *my* act, *my* will's fulfillment, *my* justification, and, therefore, *my* merit.

Following Part II of our study, we offer our concluding remarks. Therein, we review the project of the book in summary, and bring the paradox into the present-day, with the challenge of the ecumenical dialogue on this point, in the face of Christianity's conflict with contemporary cultural, moral, and religious relativism, which we have termed *Neopelagianism*.[5] Recent developments within Calvinist and Lutheran traditions, broadly considered, will be discussed, briefly, as they pertain to this issue as a subject of ecumenical dialogue.

Before we proceed, therefore, we ought to supply a brief remark about our application of the scholarly apparatus in the present work. In an effort both to keep footnotes to a minimum and to facilitate readability, we have relied heavily upon parenthetical notation for the purpose of *primary source* references. Footnotes are used to provide detailed bibliographical information where a textual citation first appears parenthetically, or to substitute for parenthetical notation where such would be unwieldy. Additionally, footnotes are used to reference secondary source material. They are also used to supply the text of the original language where a translation is offered in the body of the manuscript, and the original language is deemed important for our study—i.e. where Aquinas' writings are at issue. Footnotes are also used to make reference to texts *relevant* to an issue under discussion, but *not* necessarily in *citation* of it. Finally, footnotes are used for clarification and supplying additional details related to, but not germane to, the argument at hand.

---

5. The reason for categorizing certain strains of cultural, moral, and religious relativism together as *Neopelagianism* will be made clear later.

PART I

The Paradox of Faith and Works:

Reconciling Divine Causality with Human Free-Will and Merit

Chapter 1

Stating the Problem: Human Achievement or Divine Causality?

Were one to engage in a phenomenological investigation into human consciousness, freedom would be taken as a *given*. Human beings, in other words, do not, generally, demand *proof* that they possess the power of free-choice. Rather, we *bring this sense of ourselves with us* as we engage the world. This fact is born out in the very idea of responsibility—an idea which must be presupposed by any system of jurisprudence, and, at the interpersonal level, by any sense of *indignation* in the face of *hurt* at the hands of another.[6]

In the end, the presumption of human free-choice is so fundamental to our experience of the world that, whether or not it is a metaphysical *reality*, we cannot *function* "morally" where we do not presuppose it. In other words, in the overwhelming majority of cases, where we do not see ourselves as in some sense *responsible* for our choices, we tend not to behave with consistent affinity for the good. Rather, where we believe ourselves to lack responsibility, our behavior conforms to the chaos at the heart of the presumption of *amorality*. This is a fact of human psychology of which, as we will discuss in this chapter and the following one, both the Pelagian and the Predestinarian are aware.

As a spiritual director, Pelagius would have been faced with the *practical* problem of helping people *take responsibility* for their own choices, and *invest themselves* in the process of their own salvation. Whatever may be argued among contemporary scholars concerning

---

6. Plato addresses this issue in his *Protagoras*. There, he allows Protagoras to demonstrate that, at least *good conduct* is a matter of personal free-choice and responsibility (323^c–324^a).

Pelagius *himself*, we know that many of his *followers* strayed into heresy through adherence to his teachings. According to this heresy, human beings, under their own power, could merit salvation on account of their own good works. For the Pelagian, faith offers *assistance* in salvation by providing direction; but salvation would occur by our own power and be merited by our own "good works" *without any explicit need for divine assistance*.

For the Predestinarian, on the other hand, faith and salvation are only coincidentally related. Those who are saved are given faith, but there is no real involvement of the human person in the project of salvation. Neither act nor omission will have any effect, positive *or* negative upon our salvation, since this is granted by an *irresistible* grace, which, in a sense, "raptures"[7] the elect. This doctrine is sometimes called "double predestination" since it finally means that some are predestined for *heaven* and some for *hell*, and these decisions in no meaningful way involve the agency of the human person. "Faith" is thus reduced to the status of a sheer *gnosis*, which, as we have said, in no way involves the will's agency as an intrinsic component of the condition. This idea of *faith*, as we will see over the course of the present study, is radically different from the idea of *faith* as understood by Aquinas.[8] Why, however, do we find this conflict within the Christian tradition? What are the fundamental concerns at the heart of this paradox?

For the *Pelagian*, the difficulty lies here: if God is ultimately responsible for my ability to choose him—if he is the *direct efficient* cause, even of my free-choice for him—then there seems little meaning in the term *free-choice*, however much I may insist upon its use. It

---

7. Typically, the *a-Scriptural* term *rapture* refers to the "taking up" of the elect upon the second-coming of Christ. We apply it here, however, because of the sudden, overpowering character, and even the involuntariness, of the transformation it suggests. We hold this to be consistent with the Predestinarian view of conversion described here.

8. Classical Lutheranism, which conflates *faith* with a commitment to, and trust in, God's promise of salvation, also rejects the idea of faith as a sheer *gnosis* revelatory of one's unconditional election for salvation. Most groups descending from Calvin also conflate faith with commitment and trust; but their underlying Predestinarian premise ultimately means that even that trust and commitment proceeds in no way from within our own will, but from God's causal operation *alone*. However, see n. 112.

seems, for the Pelagian, that if God is the direct agent of choice in my election, God is the *only* agent of *real* choice in my election; and I am either *lucky* to have been saved or *unlucky* to have been damned. My salvation or damnation becomes, in the end, a kind of *sweepstakes* in which I am born "holding a number" which may or may not be found in the Book of Life from eternity.

Few people can feel inwardly responsive to a God who functions toward us in this way. Rather than leading people to engage God as a *font of mercy*, this sort of view of the divine more readily gives rise to *resentment*. A God who would create us without offering us a way to salvation (the only alternative available to us being eternal damnation) would seem cruel. For most of us, the idea of *creation for hell* is more offensive than the idea that we would simply have been *excluded from creation* in the first place. What is more, our behavior becomes motivated either by delusion or by self-service. Either we will try to avoid thinking about the possibility of our own damnation by living *as if* we are saved for certain, yet without ever really taking stock of our personal relationship with God inwardly; or else we will calculate that, since our end is already *predetermined*, and we may truly be *damned*, we ought to experience what pleasures we can while we have the chance. This problem flows so inexorably from the Predestinarian position that it finally had to be addressed by the Swiss Reformed Church in the *Second Helvetic Confession* of 1566 (X, 5.057).[9]

Little, however, could be offered in response to this difficulty. The confessors go on only to defend the importance of doctrines and of employing admonitions on the basis of their association with one's *access* to faith (X 5.057–5.060). They do *not* say that the human being actually *chooses* to respond to them with any personal assent, but that, if and only if one is predestined to be converted upon hearing them, God *causes* that conversion in association with the person's hearing "the gospel." This, likewise, is the sole character of the "power of the

---

9. The abbreviation SHC in our parenthetical citations indicates the *Second Helvetic Confession*, taken from *The Constitution of the United Presbyterian Church of the United States of America, Part I: Book of Confessions* (New York: The General Assembly of the United Presbyterian Church in the United States of America, 1967), 5.001–5.260. Citations to this text include the internal divisions of the document itself, and the standard of citation set forth in that book.

keys" and the power of "binding and loosing" in the thinking of the Helvetic confessors—the preaching of the gospel is the sole instrument, both of the *opportunity* to be forgiven, and of the *act* of repentance (XIV, 5.093–5.100). God, in other words, *causes* or *does not* cause, a person's repentance, entirely according to his own eternal decree. In the end, as the Pelagians observe, the Predestinarian thesis cannot provide any real framework for morality and personal development.

The Predestinarian, of course, objects to the Pelagian's emphasis upon personal responsibility as a *denial of God's power and sovereignty*. For the *Predestinarian*, the question of God's ultimate causality of every dimension of reality is fundamental to whether we can, in any meaningful sense, claim to be speaking of *God* at all. If we can speak of some activity which does not depend upon God, but instead requires that *God* conform to *us*—if, in other words, *God* must look *outside himself* and recognize some *objective standard* of good-conduct which *must* be rewarded—then God is decidedly *not* the source of *all* reality, since he is not the source of *that external* standard. For the Predestinarian, God is either *sovereign* or he is not; God is either *omniscient* or he is not; God is either *omnipotent* or he is not; God's choice is either *necessary* for salvation or it is *not*. For the Predestinarian, the conscious free-choice of God, who is all-powerful and all-knowing, is both *necessary* and *sufficient* for our salvation. Without him we can do nothing; *with* him, *we—human beings* with God—can do nothing. God does *everything by himself*, and we are simply *taken up* in his activity, or else left behind. To deny this, for the Predestinarian, is to deny the very nature of God.[10]

---

10. To be fair, few groups have ever been fully prepared to follow the implications of the Predestinarian claim to their ultimate logical conclusions. Most have stopped at a recognition of paradoxes which they saw no real use in attempting to resolve. Where people *have* attempted to pursue the issues, however, the results have been, from a Catholic perspective at least, truly disturbing. When the question of those who have never had opportunity to hear the gospel is posed, the *ad hoc* response is given, "We know that all the people living in that remote tribe are reprobate, because if they were not, God would have made it possible for them to have heard the gospel."

However standard this reply may be, it fails for one or the other of two reasons. Either 1) this reply rests upon the very proposition it denies, namely that the creature can resist God's grace, or else 2) it is a question-begging tautology in which we affirm that those who have not heard the gospel are lost,

The Predestinarian frames this metaphysic in the language of "sin" and "atonement." Thus, the Predestinarian tends to speak the language of *law*, whereby both *ritual strictures* and *moral standards* are treated equally. Interestingly, the Predestinarian's use of the language of *law* amounts to a dichotomy between those who are "under the law," and those who are "no-longer under the law," but "under grace"—i.e. *those who are above the law*. Those who are "under the law" are viewed as *bound* by it, since they are attempting to use the law to repay an insurmountable debt—to achieve a degree of righteousness inherently beyond their reach. This is, of course, a valid criticism of the Pelagian.

In the most radical analysis of this position, however, those "under the law"—the "unsaved"—are actually *willing evil* in the very act of attempting to obey the law (*Institutes* II.3.ii–iv),[11] which is regarded, even by the Predestinarian, as *the revelation of God's will for human conduct* (SHC XII, 5.080). The tautological reasoning runs as follows: the "unsaved" *sin* even as they *obey*, because, not having yet been freed by Christ from the dominion of Satan, they are *enslaved to sin*. On this

---

because were they to be saved, they would have heard the gospel. With the first alternative, grace must be seen as *resistible*, since it is on account of God's foreknowledge of their universal impenitence that God did not assure them access to the gospel message. Not only does this stance undermine the Predestinarian thesis, it raises the problem of attributing a cause to the divine will, rendering the divine will subject to alteration at the hands of a creature (i.e. κατά φύσις). With the second alternative, however, God's mercy is seen to know *limits*, and the Predestinarian is left to defend a thesis, perhaps at all costs, in the face of the words of Paul to Timothy, that God, "wills everyone to be saved and to come to the knowledge of the truth" (1 Tim 2:4).

Unless otherwise noted, or contained within a quotation taken from another translated source, all direct English translations of Scriptural quotations in the present work are taken from, *The Catholic Study Bible*, Donald Senior, et al. eds., The New American Bible translation, (New York: Oxford University Press, 1990). This text features the *New American Bible with Revised New Testament* © 1986, 1970 Confraternity of Christian Doctrine, Washington, DC.

11. Wherever "*Institutes*" is cited parenthetically in the present study, we refer the reader to John Calvin's *Institutes of the Christian Religion*, available in an annotated translation: J. T. McNeill, ed., *Calvin: Institutes of the Christian Religion*, translated by F. L. Battles, 2 vols. (Philadelphia: Westminster Press, 1960).

point, the *Westminster Confession* of 1646 is revealing. While the text (specifically at WCF XVI.7, 6.085)[12] does not say, in so many words, that the obedience of the "unregenerate" to the law is *inherently sinful*, it does say that, "they come short of what God requires." The presupposition in the confessors' pronouncement is that of *total depravity*. Accordingly, "Man, by his fall into a state of sin, hath wholly lost all ability of will to any spiritual good accompanying salvation (ibid. IX.3, 6.053). On the basis of this presupposition, the confessors conclude that when the "unregenerate" perform the works of the law, they are not, "done in a right manner, according to his Word; nor to a right end, the glory of God" (XVI.7, 6.085). By definition, then, *these* acts, even considered as *individual acts* apart from failures on other points of obedience, "fall short."

Up to this point, the doctrine of *total depravity* may seem consistent with Catholic teaching. Inasmuch as our inner motive for the performance of good works is something *other than* the empowering, enlivening, indwelling of the Holy Spirit in the souls of those who live the life of grace—that is to say, something other than true *charity* properly so-called—*of metaphysical necessity*, something must be lacking in our *intentionality*, and therefore, in the very *ratio* of our action and choice. A difference, in other words, of *final cause* results in a difference in *formal cause*, which means, in the final analysis (so to speak), a difference in the very *substance* of the act. From this point of view, what seems by all appearances to be a moral and ethical action, may, *on account of a certain defect of intention*, yet be *sinful* in actual fact. Aquinas, for example (*Summa Theologiae* II-II.10.iv), says that the act of an obstinate unbeliever is never strictly meritorious before God, since merit before God (which we will take up later in greater detail) depends upon grace; and obstinate unbelief stands opposed to grace. Nonetheless, he says, the obstinate unbeliever's *good acts* are not necessarily *sins*, properly speaking, *unless they proceed specifically*

---

12. In our parenthetical citations, the abbreviation WCF indicates a reference to the *Westminster Confession of Faith*. As with the *Second Helvetic Confession*, citations from the *Westminster Confession* are taken from *The Constitution of the United Presbyterian Church of the United States of America, Part I: Book of Confessions* [6.001–6.178], and include the internal divisions of the document itself, as well as the standard of citation set forth in that book.

from the agent's unbelief as his motive for action, in which case, these *materially* good acts are *formally* evil.[13] However, a closer look at the arguments at hand reveals a profound point of departure between the Westminster confessors and the Catholic Church on the question of the nature and extent of human depravity in the fallen state.

According to the Westminster confessors, as we have said, outside the context of grace, the human being, "hath wholly lost all ability of will to *any* spiritual good *accompanying* salvation" (ibid. IX.3, 6.053). For Catholics, this statement is far too broad; for it would seem to

---

13. Let us consider, for instance, the case of the so-called *active nihilist*. The *nihilist* is one who, as Nietzsche suggests, has come to reject any absolute, objective moral framework—any *Logos* according to which truth and falsehood, right and wrong, good or evil can be measured. Life, in other words, has no objective meaning or value. The sole responsibility for valuing belongs to the one who possesses the power of choice and agency. No reference is made to any transcendent valuer or giver of meaning. "God," in other words, "is dead" (*The Gay Science* #125). As Nietzsche's madman understands, however, the acceptance of *nihilism* is no trivial matter. Few have the inner constitution to face a world devoid of absolute moral value. The *passive nihilist*, then, is one who denies the Absolute, and goes on to live (or perhaps to die) in a way consistent with this denial—that is to say, *as if life has no meaning*. The *active nihilist*, by contrast, is the so-called *übermensch* or *over-man*, who goes on to create his or her own *self-grounded* world of meaning through a sheer *act of will*—that is to say, a *will to power*. The *active nihilist*, then, may choose a "moral" action, not out of some interior (if however unconscious) assent to an inviolable truth, innate dignity, or for-its-own-sake value, but out of this self-aggrandizing *will to power*—whereby the choice is made on the terms of the *willer alone*, as the sole moral "absolute"—for *this* alternative over its contrary.

Whatever the *matter* of the chosen moral object, therefore, the *formal* character of the act is, from any authentically Judeo-Christian point of view, fundamentally sinful; for it rests in the presumption that the human being, rather than God, is the author of moral value. This stance is, in the end, no new thing at all, but the *original* sin depicted in the story of the Fall in the third chapter of Genesis, where the serpent says (v. 5), "No, God knows well that the moment you eat of it your eyes will be opened and you will be like gods who know what is good and what is bad," or more literally, "you will be like God who knows what is good and what is evil." In other words, the serpent suggests that the man and the woman might choose to be like gods in *the way in which* they know what is good and what is evil—that is to say, *by defining the parameters of the moral universe*.

exclude even *personal immortality of the soul* from the possible objects of will available to those in a state of sin. Personal immortality of the soul is clearly a *spiritual* good (though not, properly speaking, a *supernatural* one), insofar as it refers, not to the bodily good, but to the good of the *separated soul* after the body has died; and it is a good that, while insufficient to *cause* or to *constitute* salvation, most certainly *accompanies* it. A Catholic critique, however, must go further than this. The Westminster confessors, maintain that those who are "no-longer under the law"—those who have been *freed* by the power of God—cannot be *sentenced* under the law, even should they sin, because they exist outside sin's jurisdiction. This claim amounts, therefore, to a radical separation between the *human agent* and the life of grace under which that human agent is subsumed. If by *sin* we mean *an act of will whereby the human person stands apart from God's grace*, we are, from the perspective of the Westminster confessors, wholly *incapable* of committing it, once saved, *no matter what* our inner disposition or exterior action—and *this* idea, the Catholic Church rejects.

Of course, it is generally maintained, even by the Predestinarian, that the law is not wholly *abrogated* (SHC XII, 5.085; WCF XIX.6, 6.098–6.099). There is still, at least in theory, some acknowledgement that a certain standard of conduct is to be maintained. For many, general, albeit imperfect, conformity to this standard is taken as evidence of one's election, where it is confessed to proceed from one's faith in Christ. It is admitted, however, that the "saved" no longer incur any *spiritual* penalty for violations of the law. In practice, therefore, this tends to promote a general sense that the law *no longer frames our lives*. Practices of fasting, ritual cleansing laws, circumcision, and dietary restrictions, for example, are no longer viewed as *normative*, and are frequently viewed as *sinful denials* of Christ's liberating activity. Frequently, this can result in the deterioration of *any* framework within which one's transformation in Christ can be made manifest, even to oneself. As a consequence, we tend, again, to return to the problem of relying upon a sheer *gnosis* that *we* are saved; and the aphorism is heard, "though I should die in the arms of a prostitute, I know that I am saved through faith in Christ."

Chapter 2

A History of the Faith-Works Controversy

In the question of the precise nature of the relationship, for Christianity, between faith and human salvation, the two extremes among possible responses are represented, as we have said, by the positions of the Predestinarians (such as John Calvin and the Westminster Confessors) and the Pelagians, respectively (discussed in overview in Chapter 1). The struggle between these two extremes has been a perennial one for the Church,[14] dealt with in some way by every major systematician. Further, it continues to be a point of dispute today, between Protestants and Catholics. The positions articulated by the Pelagians and the Reformation-era Predestinarians, respectively, are in no way exclusively their own. Both strains of thought have been found within the Christian community from the earliest days of the Church. They can be seen throughout the New Testament, as, for example, in the tension between the treatment of law in the Gospel of Matthew and in the writings of Paul, respectively; in Paul's chastisements both of legalism and gnosticism within the communities under his care; and in the balanced view of the interplay of faith and works found in James and Hebrews. Augustine dealt with Pelagianism proper in the fifth century; but his own responses give rise to certain extreme interpretations as those which played so great a role in the thought of Martin Luther, and

---

14. Even in the Apostolic Age, Christianity faced the difficulty of reconciling these extremes in essence, i.e. in the case of the disputes between the Jewish Christians, on the one hand, and the Gnosticizers, on the other. While the intensity of this basic dispute has waxed and waned over the centuries, it has never wholly vanished in any historical period in the life of the Church, as we will see in the body of this chapter.

even more so in that of John Calvin, leading to the Protestant schisms of the sixteenth century. The discussions of this issue over the course of the Catholic Church's *internal*[15] reformation again led to conflict. This conflict was serious enough to compel Pope Clement VIII, in 1598, to convene the *Congregatio de Auxiliis* in the hope of thrashing out the paradox to Catholic satisfaction once and for all. This effort ended without success after nine years, when the *Congregatio* was closed in 1607 by Pope Paul V,[16] offering a brief reprieve before the emergence of Jansensim. In this chapter we present a concise historical overview of this faith-works controversy, broadly considered,[17] briefly surveying each moment outlined above, from the apostolic era's tensions, to the *Congregatio de Auxiliis* and its aftermath.

THE APOSTOLIC AGE:
LEGALISM VS. GNOSTICISM IN THE NEW TESTAMENT

While we must be careful not to paint with too broad a brush, we can distill the apostolic-era *gnostic vs. legalist* controversy this way: while a) some, who lacked mystical or ecstatic experience, felt unduly bound to the meticulous practice of the law; b) others, who claimed to have had mystical or ecstatic experiences, tended to feel unduly privileged with a revelation of personal salvation not sensed by their counterparts. The *legalists*, for their part, tended, in practice, to *underplay* the sig-

---

15. We prefer to avoid the term *Counter-Reformation* because of its pejorative connotations. It takes for granted that the "Reformers" were decidedly *right*, not only in their own theological claims, but in their understanding of the theological claims made by the Catholic Church, and that the Catholic Church sought to suppress truth and *cling to error*.

16. If one can point to any "triumph" in the conflict ended by Paul V, it is the sheer *avoidance of disaster*. Unlike most other conflicts waged over similar issues in this period, the *Congregatio De Auxiliis* did *not*, itself, end in schism.

17. A more detailed discussion of this history, stopping, however, in the modern period, can be found in Dom M. John Farrelly, O.S.B., *Predestination, Grace, and Free Will* (Westminster, Maryland: The Newman Press, 1964), 1–151.

nificance of Jesus' advent upon the historico-salvific scene, depending for their salvation, instead, upon the practice of the law more or less exactly as it had been before, as if with Christ, nothing had really changed at all. Thus, in the Apostolic and Patristic periods, the legalists were known as "Judaizers" for their failure to recontextualize the Mosaic legal tradition within the New Covenant of Christ's grace.[18] The *gnosticizers*, however, tended to feel exempted from the traditional Jewish-now-Christianized moral standards, their community's liturgical norms and rubrics, and in extreme cases, the very theological foundation of the faith to which their original experience had been attributed. Evidence of this *gnostic vs. legalist* conflict can be found, as we have said, throughout the New Testament.[19] These gnosticizing influences had a serious impact upon the thinking of Christians within the mainstream of orthodoxy—an influence which early Christian writers attempted to reverse.

Matthew's Gospel contains evidence of this tension. There, the figure of Jesus simply cannot be properly understood outside the context of a

---

18. John speaks to this point in the prologue of his Gospel, where he distinguishes between the Old Covenant of the law and the New Covenant of grace. He writes, "From his fullness we have all received, grace in place of grace, because while the law was given through Moses, grace and truth came through Jesus Christ" (1:16–17). By contrast, Eusebius (*Church History* III.27) speaks of the Ebionites, who held a low Christology, and followed the rubrics of the rabbinical law, not only unchanged, but without any substantial recontextualization. See, however, n. 28 in the present study. For Eusebius' *Church History*, the reader may consult, for convenience, Eusebius, *The Church History of Eusebius*, Rev. Arthur Cushman McGiffert, Ph.D., trans., in, Schaff, Philip, D.D., LL.D., and Henry Wace, D.D., eds., *A Select Library of Nicene and Post-Nicene Fathers of the Christian Church* (Second Series), vol. I, (New York: The Christian Literature Company, 1890), 1–403. For III.27, consult 158–160.

19. We are concerned here, however, *not* so much with any particular *gnostic sect* as such, but with general *gnosticizing tendencies* discernable within the larger Christian community. For our purposes in this discussion, we will define as *gnosticizing tendencies*, those theological leanings which tend toward a claim that salvation is granted to the elect along with a revelation of *eternal security* and a consequent *immunity* from all personal responsibility for one's own participation as a *willing agent* who can be held *morally accountable* for the actions and omissions flowing from personal choice.

legal framework of some kind. The role he exercises in *redefining the pure state of the law* in Chapters 5–7 requires the affirmation that some legal framework *persists* from Judaism in Matthew's view of Church. Thus, we read:

> Do not think that I have come to abolish the law or the prophets. I have come not to abolish but to fulfill. Amen, I say to you, until heaven and earth pass away, not the smallest letter or the smallest part of a letter will pass from the law, until all things have taken place. Therefore, whoever breaks[20] one of the least of these commandments and teaches others to do so will be called least in the kingdom of heaven. But whoever obeys and teaches these commandments will be called greatest in the kingdom of heaven. (5:17–19)

Matthew is interested in the purification of the law for the new Covenant. Jesus criticizes the Pharisees, who had mastered the technique of *bending* and *shaping* the law for their own purposes, without actually "breaking" the so-called "letter" of it. Jesus' use, in verse 18, of grammatical references to the written law[21] speaks precisely to this metaphor; the Covenantal law is to be kept to the smallest detail. Again, he criticizes the Pharisees for manipulating the law to serve their own purposes—making it *harsh* when harsh works well for *them*, but *loose* when loose works well for *them*. Once the law is purified by Jesus, it will be strictly maintained in its new perfection. The power of "binding and loosing" (cf. 16:19; 18:18), therefore, is not about holding fast to points of the purified law or relaxing them. It does, of course, clearly entail the authority to establish disciplinary and ritual norms for the Covenantal community, based upon the purified law; but this is merely a practical requirement for the actual *exercise* of the power of "binding and loosing." First and foremost, therefore, the

---

20. The Greek λύω (or λύση as in this grammatical context) is translated here as "break," but it would be better, given the context here, and elsewhere in this Gospel (16:13–20; 18:15–18; 28:18–20), to render this word "relax," "loosen," or "overlook".

21. That is to say, the silent *iota subscript* and a κεραία (*keraia*), meaning a *stroke*—i.e., *a single movement of the pen in the writing-out of a textual character*.

power of "binding and loosing" is a *charism*. Those who receive it are charged with holding people *accountable* to the purified law itself, which *cannot* be relaxed, and then, upon convicting them to repentance, *releasing them* again into the Covenantal life, which is to be lived without compromise. All of this, of course, *presupposes* the law's *purity*, established, as we have said, in chapters 5–7 of Matthew's text.

Throughout Matthew's Gospel, therefore, followers of Christ are held to be *morally accountable* for their own conduct relative to the call of Christ to live the Covenantal life of the kingdom. This is part and parcel of Matthew's use of the term ἐκκλησία (*ekkleisia*) where he promised the establishment of his post-resurrectional earthly reign (16:13–20).[22] This reading is clear in light of 25:31–46, where Christ contrasts the saved from the damned in his discourse on the Final Judgment. There we read:

> When the Son of Man comes in his glory, and all the angels with him, he will sit upon his glorious throne, and all the nations will be assembled before him. And he will separate them one from another, as a shepherd separates the sheep from the goats. He will place the sheep on his right and the goats on his left. Then the king will say to those on his right, "Come, you who are blessed by my Father. Inherit the kingdom prepared for you

---

22. The Greek ἐκκλησία (or in this grammatical context, ἐκκλησίαν) derives from the prefix ἐκ or ἐξ, denoting an origin, in the sense of *from* or *out*, and the word καλέω, that is: *to call, to call forth, to call by name, to call as if by name*. This root word καλέω must be understood in light of Jesus' authoritative discourse in chapters 5–7. Given these passages in Matthew's Gospel, his use of the term ἐκκλησία at 16:18 and twice again at 18:17, should be understood from within the context of a word family which includes not only καλέω, but also καλεύω, that is: *to order, to command, to issue a commandment*.

Admittedly, only at 8:18, 15:35, 18:25, and 27:64, does Matthew use the term καλέω, using the term ἐντολή to mean *commandments of religious law*. Still, the two concepts are not altogether different. The term καλεύω seems to suggest the issuance of an *isolated* commandment in the sense of an *order* or a *juridical decree* (i.e. to go now and do some particular thing), while the term ἐντολή (as in 5:19, for example: ἐντολῶν) indicates a *precept* to be observed *for all time* (see n. 20). Indeed, Jesus associates obedience to the law (ὁ νόμος), in the form of keeping commandments (ἐντολή), with righteousness (δικαιουσύνη) at 5:17–20.

from the foundation of the world. For I was hungry and you gave me food, I was thirsty and you gave me drink, a stranger and you welcomed me, naked and you clothed me, ill and you cared for me, in prison and you visited me." Then the righteous will answer him and say, "Lord, when did we see you hungry and feed you, or thirsty and give you drink? When did we see you a stranger and welcome you, or naked and clothe you? When did we see you ill or in prison, and visit you?" And the king will say to them in reply, "Amen, I say to you, whatever you did for one of these least brothers of mine, you did for me." Then he will say to those on his left, "Depart from me, you accursed, into the eternal fire prepared for the devil and his angels. For I was hungry and you gave me no food, I was thirsty and you gave me no drink, a stranger and you gave me no welcome, naked and you gave me no clothing, ill and in prison, and you did not care for me." Then they will answer and say, "Lord, when did we see you hungry or thirsty or a stranger or naked or ill or in prison, and not minister to your needs?" He will answer them, "Amen, I say to you, what you did not do for one of these least ones, you did not do for me." And these will go off to eternal punishment, but the righteous to eternal life.

The phraseology at verse 34, of course, requires comment. Here, Jesus says, "Inherit the kingdom prepared for you *from the foundation of the world.*" The Predestinarian will, of course, argue that this passage simply asserts that those who are saved from eternity will behave in ways consistent with God's righteousness, while the reprobate will, in turn, behave accordingly. This reading, however, is unsatisfactory. It trivializes the *insistent detail* of the account—"hungry or thirsty or a stranger or naked or ill or in prison" (v. 44). This detail is covered in *two* dialogues within the discourse as a whole—once for those on his *right* and once for those on his *left*—and appears twice *within* each of those dialogues. This indicates, clearly and emphatically, the *intentionality* of the standard of judgment here presented to the audience. Furthermore, the Predestinarian language employed in this narrative does not suggest the so-called *hard predestination* or *absolute predestination* of individual persons, but the eternal will of God to welcome the righteous, *whomever they may be,* into eternal glory. Precisely to make this point, Jesus speaks, in verse 32, of the judgement of *nations*—that is, *people who live according to a common ethos*. The Nation of Israel, in other words, is *the communion of those who share in the Covenantal life*. In this account, therefore, Jesus makes a statement about the requirements of the Covenantal life of the kingdom, and what God has planned, from eternity, to do for those who remain true to that life. Clearly, Matthew's presentation of this discourse suggests something far more than a merely *coincidental* relationship between righteousness and good works, as we see, again, at 16:27, where Jesus declares, "The Son of Man will come with his angels in his Father's glory, and then he will repay everyone according to his conduct." As Matthew presents the gospel, it is clear that *self-identification* as a Christian is simply not enough for our salvation. Given grace, we must go on to *do* something in conformity to the will of God the Father. At 7:21, Jesus makes this point unambiguously, saying, "Not everyone who says to me, 'Lord, Lord,' will enter the kingdom of heaven, but only the one who does the will of my Father in heaven."

Contrarily, however, if one pays inadequate attention to the larger Tradition within the New Testament, one can easily (and many do) read *Paul* as denying *any* authority structure within the Church, and any *salvific necessity* for continuing and developing personally within the life of grace. This reading of Paul is, as we have said, *easy*; but it is *superficial*. In reality, Paul writes in *legal* terms to those who understand the *language* of law.[23] His emphasis is placed upon the liberation Christ provides from the bondage of sin, and the fact that this liberation is provided through a work of grace *we cannot bring about for ourselves*—neither through our own unaided power, nor under our

---

23. The Romans understood the language of law as U.S. citizens understand the language of rights. Just as "rights-talk" is used wherever a rhetorician wishes to appeal to a contemporary U.S. citizen, so "law-talk" communicated the message of the gospel to the Romans in language *they* would understand, and to which they would respond. In his use of "law-talk" with the Galatians, however, Paul uses a different approach. He does not speak in the *juridical* language of Rome, but in the *Covenantal* language of the Levites. The law of the Old Covenant differed from the legal system of Rome in that the legal system of Rome is merely a *political* structure, while Hebrew Covenantal law was also a *ritual* structure bound up with the act of *worship*. We err in our interpretation of Paul to the degree that we neglect this distinction.

own authority.[24] Paul does not seem interested in the complexities of the theological question concerning merit *within* an unmerited life of grace; nor does he seem to concern himself with the psychologico-metaphysical complexities involved in one's *initial* response to the grace-offering of Christ.[25]

Perhaps the clearest examples of Paul's emphasis upon moral order[26] within the life of grace can be found in his Corinthian correspondence. There, Paul confronts the gnosticizing tendencies within this never-Jewish community, wherein no regard for the Rabbinical *moral* tradition informed the community's sensibilities for good or ill. In the absence of this tradition, the Corinthian community saw its Christianity purely in terms of *faith* without reference to any ritual purity or work of righteousness.[27]

---

24. The language Paul employs elsewhere, when speaking about the proper conduct and disposition of one *living-out* the life of grace shows some sensibility in favor of *obedience* (Eph 5:21; Phil 2:12; Col 3:18–4:1) ritual practice (1 Cor 11:2–14:40), inter-personal responsibility (Gal 6:1–10; Col 3:12–17; 2 Cor 13:11–12), and dissociation from a former way of life (Eph 4:17–5:20, 6:10–18; Col 3:1–11; 1 Thess 4:1–8; 2 Thess 3:6–13). In other words, even for Paul, it seems that while the gift of forgiveness cannot be *merited*, it comes with a requirement that we *respond* to Christ's act of mercy and generosity through a self-dedication to him in a *life of service* to his work.

25. Disputes emerged on these questions in later ages; but the disputants' employment of Paul's writings as "proof texts" in an effort to resolve them represents, we contend, a misuse of his work.

26. Liturgical order was also at issue in Corinth. See n. 27.

27. See Eusebius, *Church History* IV.23.i–ii. It is clear upon any reading of the Corinthian literature that they were a morally and ritually disordered community. In the time of Paul, Corinth had no resident bishop, but seems to have been governed remotely by Paul himself, and subsequently by the bishops of Rome, at least through the time of Clement. This point is made by Raymond E. Brown, S.S. in *Priest and Bishop: Biblical Reflections* (New York: Paulist Press, 1970), 70–72. There, Brown points out that the overwhelming attention paid by Paul to the Corinthian Community is due, not to its *model* status as a community without a bishop of its own, but to its *failure* as an *experimental* or *half-formed structure* in contrast to Philippi, for example, where a bishop governed the community *locally*. With neither the heritage of the Jewish law, nor the governance of a resident bishop, the Corinthian community could not locate for itself a workable framework within which to govern their own moral

When Paul writes to the Galatians, however, he must urge them *off* the strict *rubrics of the law*. Had the Galatian church been composed strictly of Jewish converts, they might well have continued indefinitely practicing the rabbinical law, requiring circumcision, observing the customary feasts, and so forth.[28] The presence of gentile converts within the community, however, raised important questions concerning

and ritual behavior.

28. In the Syrian Jacobite Church, the Mosaic dietary laws are still observed. In both the Coptic and Ethiopian churches, circumcision is still practiced prior to baptism, and the Mosaic dietary restrictions are observed, especially as concerns the consumption of certain animals. The Ethiopian Church distinguishes between clean and unclean meats, observes days of ritual purification, and keeps a kind of *dual Sabbath* on both Saturday *and* Sunday. These Churches all separated from the larger Church early, following the Council of Chalcedon (A.D. 451) which they rejected, earning the title "monophysites," for their insistence upon a *one-natured* Christ. As appears in nearly all cases in which churches in true apostolic succession separate from the larger Church, they remained largely *as they were* at the time of schism. This fact suggests that the Jewishness of the early Church, even toward the end of the patristic period, was prominent in many places. The Semitic heritage of these churches, especially of the Coptic and Ethiopian churches, makes it likely that these regions were not so much "converted" to Christianity, but *organically fulfilled* with Christianity's arrival at the hands of missionary apostles. The Coptic Church, for example, likely received the gospel with the hands of the great Jewish *diaspora* at Alexandria (see Eusebius, *Church History* II.16–17), and over time, expanded from this inception, ultimately embracing the indigenous Egyptians, who, today, overwhelmingly constitute the church's ethnic majority. That these communities would, therefore, *remain* essentially Jewish in their observance of the law, even as they assimilated gentile converts, seems natural; and reveals that there is nothing inherently contradictory between faith in Christ and some form of legal observance. For more on these churches, see Donald Attwater, *The Dissident Eastern Churches* (Milwaukee: The Bruce Publishing Company, 1937), especially pp. 235–269. For more on the Copts, specifically, consult Mark Gruber, O.S.B., *Journey Back to Eden: My Life and Times among the Desert Fathers*, M. Michele Ransil, C.D.P., ed. (Maryknoll, New York: Orbis Books, 2002); and Mark Gruber, O.S.B., *Sacrifice in the Desert: A Study of an Egyptian Minority Through the Prism of Coptic Monasticism*, M. Michele Ransil, C.D.P., ed. (Lanham, MD: University Press of America, 2003).

the relationship between *ritual* practice and *grace*.[29] Paul argues at the Council of Jerusalem (Acts 15:1–29), that circumcision need not be *imposed* upon gentile converts, since it is not the *cause* of our salvation. Ritual practice, in other words, is not salvific *in-and-of itself*. Rather, it is a *facilitator* of our *relationship with God*. Insofar as ritual practice serves to help us respond more fully to the grace-offering of Christ, it is good, and even *necessary* for our salvation. But insofar as it becomes a stumbling-block to that relationship, it becomes a stumbling-block to our *salvation*, and must be jettisoned. Nonetheless, as Paul makes clear in 1 Corinthians 13:1–13, certain moral requirements for the Covenantal life with God are taken seriously, and must be understood to be in some way relevant to the question of personal salvation. Paul suggests this much at 2 Corinthians 13:1–10. There, he writes of his impending need to impose discipline upon a community whose devotion to the Covenantal life is questionable, in light of the *conduct* of the people. He stresses the persistence they manifest in their disregard for the norms of the Covenantal life, in spite of repeated warnings (vv. 1–2), stressing the authority he enjoys, as an apostle, to hold the community accountable to those norms. He exhorts them, as he writes:

> Examine yourselves to see whether you are living in faith. Test yourselves. Do you not realize that Jesus Christ is in you?—unless, of course, you fail the test. I hope you will discover that we have not failed. But we pray to God that you may not do evil, not that we may appear to have passed the test but that you may do what is right, even though we may seem to have failed. For we cannot do anything against the truth, but only for the truth. For we rejoice when we are weak but you are strong. What we pray for is your improvement.

---

29. Whether the community had been essentially Jewish or essentially gentile at its founding is irrelevant for our discussion here. The point is that, early on, the community became ethnically mixed, and because of a powerful influence from Judeo-Christian legalists, faced a consequent crisis regarding the proper parameters of the law within the context of the New Covenant of Christ's grace. Nonetheless, as a point of history, the *Galatians*, as such, were gentiles; indeed, they are the group of migrants whose descendants became the *Gaels* of Gaul, and the *Celts* of the Gaelic regions of Scotland and Ireland. They had lived in Asia Minor since around the third century B.C.

I am writing this while I am away, so that when I come I may
not have to be severe in virtue of the authority that the Lord has
given me to build up and not to tear down. (vv. 5–10)[30]

Paul is concerned, here, with lifting the people up from a condition of superficial association with the Covenant of Christ, dissociated from any interior transformation. Instead, he insists that he has fulfilled his charge as an apostle, when his people are so fully conformed to the Covenantal norms that they do not need his imposition of coercive authority. If they are strong in their Covenantal lives, then he can be weak in his exercise of coercive power; but as long as they remain weak, or even lifeless, he will show his strength as an apostle of Christ, reprimanding them with severity when he comes in judgment over them. This tells us that, as Paul understands the matter, the life of the Covenant is about far more than a mere annunciation of belief, or a momentary, transitory experience of conviction and repentance. The life of the Covenant must be lived out with constancy in our conduct, lest, failing this test, Jesus Christ is not in us, any longer.

James, however, is no doubt the clearest of all New Testament witnesses, not only to the salvific relevance of *morality*, but also to the reality of *merit* in human agency. He insists, not only upon *faith*, but upon *lived faith*; and he is *not* simply talking about the *signs* of true faith, but of *gaining merit before God* through our efforts-in-grace. At 1:22 and 25, he writes:

> Be doers of the word and not hearers only, deluding yourselves.... [T]he one who peers into the perfect law of freedom and perseveres, and is not a hearer who forgets but a doer who acts, such a one *shall be blessed in what he does.*[31]

Again, at 2:12–13, he cautions, "So speak and so act as people who will be judged by the law of freedom. For the judgment is merciless to one who has not shown mercy; mercy triumphs over justice." His strongest words in favor of the necessity of works to bring the grace of faith to fruition, however, come at 2:14–26. There he writes:

---

30. My *emphasis*.
31. My *emphasis*.

> What good is it, my brothers, if someone has faith but does not have works? Can that faith save him? If a brother or sister has nothing to wear and has no food for the day, and one of you says to them, "Go in peace, keep warm, and eat well," but you do not give them the necessities of the body, what good is it? So also, faith itself, if it does not have works, is dead.
>
> Indeed someone might say, "You have faith and I have works." Demonstrate your faith to me without works, and I will demonstrate my faith to you from my works. You believe that God is one. You do well. Even the demons believe that and tremble. Do you want proof, you ignoramus, that faith without works is useless? Was not Abraham our father justified by works when he offered his son Isaac upon the altar? You see that faith was active along with his works, and faith was *completed by* the works. *Thus* the Scripture was fulfilled that says, "Abraham believed God, and it was credited to him as righteousness," and he was called "the friend of God." See how a person is justified by works and *not by faith alone*. And in the same way, was not Rahab the harlot also justified by works when she welcomed the messengers and sent them out by a different rout? For just as a body without a spirit is dead, so also faith without works is dead.[32]

Clearly, James sees *works* not only as an *indicator* of our righteousness, but as a necessary response to God's grace, without which the grace of the Covenant cannot endure in us. This is because Covenant is about *relationship*, and is thus *dialogical*. The Covenant, in other words, is a *friendship* (v. 23); and *friendship* can be *turned away*. At 1:14–15, James points out that "each person is tempted when he is lured and enticed by his own desire. Then desire conceives and brings forth sin, and when sin reaches maturity it gives birth to death." His point here is that a *turning inward* to one's own desires, rather than outward to the desires of God,[33] represents nothing less than a *rejection of the gift of God's friendship* and thus, of his *saving grace*.

---

32. My *emphasis*.

33. James describes as the *purity of religion* that the widows and orphans should be fed (1:27).

It is difficult to suggest any reading of James on this point that could possibly support the *eternal security* thesis maintained by the Predestinarian. Clearly, for James, righteousness can be *lost*. But what does this have to do with *merit*? James clearly associates the ability to turn *from* grace with the contrary ability to turn *toward* it. He makes this clear at 5:16, 19–20, where he writes:

> Therefore, confess your sins to one another and pray for one another, that you may be healed. . . .
> My brothers, if anyone among you should stray from the truth and someone bring him back, he should know that whoever brings back a sinner from the error of his way *will save his soul from death and will cover a multitude of sins.*[34]

There can be no doubt that, for James, works *gain an increase in graces from God*—they *merit* before him through the *righteousness* (v. 16) which first comes to the human person as a free gift from God (1:16–17).

A view similar to James' is found in Hebrews, at 6:4–8. There, a clear connection is made between human conduct and preservation of a life of grace:

> [I]t is impossible in the case of those who have once been enlightened and tasted the heavenly gift and shared in the holy Spirit and tasted the good word of God and the powers of the age to come, and *then* have *fallen away*, to bring them to repentance again, since they are recrucifying the Son of God for themselves and holding him up to contempt. Ground that has absorbed the rain falling upon it repeatedly and brings forth crops useful to those for whom it is cultivated *receives a blessing from God*. But if it produces thorns and thistles, it is rejected; it will soon be cursed and finally burned.[35]

---

34. My *emphasis*.

35. My *emphasis*. Upon a close reading of this passage, the author does not seem to be suggesting that a person can never be forgiven of a sin after baptism, but that we can harden our hearts so thoroughly as to be, for all intents and purposes, unreachable. This is the plight of the damned, and my be understood as a reference to the so-called "sin against the Holy Spirit." The metaphor of "repeated rains" (v. 7) may refer to an early form of the sacrament of recon-

The point is that the availability of grace comports an obligation to *respond* with a *lived-faith* manifest in good works. He goes on to say at verses 9–10:

> But we are sure in your regard, beloved, of better things related to salvation, even though we speak in this way. For God is not unjust so as to *overlook your work and the love you have demonstrated for his name by having served* and continuing to serve the holy ones.[36]

When all is said and done, the New Testament read in a vacuum leaves the *precise nature* of the relationship between human free-will and divine causality in the realm of *mystery*. What is clear, however, from a nuanced reading, is the fact that human beings are powerless to save themselves by any effort of their own, and yet are held responsible for whether or not they live in a state of grace. This paradox leaves us to draw one of two conclusions: either 1) We are all born guilty, and thus *morally reprobate*, i.e. morally responsible for our gracelessness, while God saves some and not others, *entirely at his own whim*; or else 2) we are all born outside the life of grace, but are all *offered* grace by Christ, and *rendered capable* by God of freely choosing to *accept* that grace or to *reject* it, thus *assuming moral responsibility* for this "free-gift" life of grace. In the early Church, the first of these options was the stock-in-trade of the gnostic sects, and represented a power-play on the part of gnostic ascetics who set themselves up as the "chosen few," God's elect—superior by God's choice. The second option was that which ultimately came to be recognized as "orthodoxy," and which continues to find affirmation today in the teachings of the Catholic Church, and the churches of the East.[37]

---

ciliation, which, as suggested in John's Gospel (13:1–15), may have involved the washing of feet. Alternatively, it may refer to repeated exhortations from a spiritual father or the church leadership, or even repeated participation in Eucharistic communion. Again, John's Gospel suggests this metaphor when, at Cana, ritual cleansing jars are filled with *water* only to have that water transformed into *fine wine* (2:1–11).

36. My *emphasis*.

37. By contrast, the "chosen few" of orthodoxy (the *ordained*) are the *guardians* of the New Law, who themselves, have *no special knowledge* con-

The Controversy between Augustine and Pelagianism

By the late Patristic period, the question of divine causality vs. human free-will and merit began to take doctrinal shape. This occurred as an indirect result of Augustine's polemic against the Manichees. In his writings against that decidedly gnostic, quasi-Christian sect, he placed emphasis upon the goodness of the human free-will. This was an important point for Augustine to pursue against the Manichees, because as *metaphysical dualists*, they rejected as evil anything connected with corporeal existence.[38] As a *Christian*, the deepest implications of an authentic understanding of the *Incarnation* were at stake. The sacramental life itself is, at least in part, a *corporeal* life; and authentic

---

cerning their own salvation, nor any special right to it by virtue of the dignity of their office.

38. See *Retractions* I.9.i–ii. The Manichees, of which Augustine had been an "auditor" or *cateheumen*, were an antisacramental gnostic sect resembling, in their basic mythology, Zoroastrianism. Mani, who had founded the sect, had once belonged to a baptist community known as the Mughtasilas until, after receiving a *gnosis*, he came to reject the efficacy of the baptismal ritual. While, today, little can be said with certainty concerning the Mughtasilas, the Manichaeans' easy intercourse with Jewish and Christian references, as well as with Zoroastrianism, provide grounds for the suggestion that the Mughtasilas sect was itself, an outgrowth of the still-extant, though little-known, Mandaean sect. Like the Mughtasilas, and the Mandaeans, the Manichean's origins are Near-Eastern; Mani's writings (preserved now only in fragments) are composed in Aramaic. Interestingly, the name *Mandaean* derives from the Aramaic, *maddā'* or *mandā'*, meaning *knowledge*, and thus indicates their fundamentally *gnostic* belief-system. This sect is also known as the *Ṣabaeans* or *Baptizers*, and the *Naṣoraeans*—a name which likely derives from the *Nazirite vow* of ritual purity described in Numbers 6:1–12. This vow was taken by figures such as Samson (Judges 13–16), seemingly Paul (Acts 18:18; 21:23–24), and perhaps John the Baptist. For more on the Manichaeans, see J. Ries, "Manichaeism," in NCE, vol. IX: 153–160. Ries, there, supports the notion that the Mughtasilas may have been related to the Mandaeans (153). For a brief discussion of the Mandaeans, see "Mandaeans," *The HarperCollins Dictionary of Religion*, Jonathan Z. Smith, et. al., eds., (New York: HarperSanFrancisco, 1995), 678–679; and G. W. Macrae, "Mandaean Religion," in NCE, vol. IX: 145.

Christianity promises the *resurrection of the body* on the last day. Part and parcel of this manner of existence is the human free-will, which can choose to *remain bound* inordinately to transitory realities, or else to *contextualize those realities* in light of eternity. In this way, the human person, acting *here and now* is not *doomed* to an evil existence as a corporeal entity, but can, with the help of grace, achieve righteousness in this life through the exercise of his will in a choice *for* freedom, and *against* bondage.

To Augustine's dismay, however, his writings were employed by Pelagius in support of Pelagius' own thesis concerning human freedom—a thesis Augustine vehemently rejected. According to Pelagius, human beings were *born* with a free-will which could be employed, even in this purely natural condition, in the performance of meritorious good acts, or by contrast, in *de*meritorious *evil* acts. By meriting according to one's good works, one would become *righteous*, and, in essence, *earn* God's approval, achieving eternal life in heaven. Pelagius employed Augustine's writings in his own defense, noting that in *De Libero Arbitrio*, Augustine *did not speak frequently of grace.*

Augustine, however, rejected any association with Pelagius, retorting that while he did mention grace in his treatise against the Manichees, he did not labor heavily upon precisely *that* issue because, *grace* was not *at* issue in that discussion (*Retractions* I.9.iv), where the goodness of the created order was the subject of dispute (ibid. I.9.i). Indeed, stressed Augustine, the sheer *novelty* of the Pelagian heresy had been unthinkable to him at the time he had written *De Libero Arbitrio*, such that he could not have imagined that any *overt* mention of the necessity of grace in human meriting could reasonably have been *required* of him in his attempt to preserve orthodoxy. He expected his reader, in other words, to take the necessity of grace as a *given*—as an unquestioned foundation upon which any Christian thesis rests. Much of Augustine's *subsequent* work, then, stressed the necessity of grace weightily, *because* of the Pelagian heresy; and this emphasis came, at times, at the expense of an adequate defense of human free-will.

Nonetheless, Augustine's writings *as a whole* reveal a clear struggle to *make sense* of this paradox. In his *De Diversus Quaestionibus* I.1–2, he struggles palpably to articulate this mystery as it manifests itself in Romans 7:7–25, and 9:10–29. As we considered earlier, Paul's discussion, in those passages, concerns the relationship of the law to grace, and in what sense the law could be understood as *good*, while at the same time, it made sin *abound*. For Augustine, the answer to this question rests somehow in the bondage of the human will outside the context of grace. He writes:

> [T]he law cannot be fulfilled except by spiritual persons, and there cannot be such save by grace. The more one is assimilated to the spiritual law, the more one attains to a spiritual disposition, the more one fulfills the law. (ibid I.7)[39]

Augustine elaborates upon this claim, with an explanation the Catholic Church has never endorsed without some qualification. He writes:

> [A]ctual willing is certainly within our power; that it is not within our power to do that which is good is part of the deserts of original sin. This is not the original nature of man, but the penalty of his guilt, whereby mortality was brought in as a second nature, from which the grace of our Creator sets us free, if we submit ourselves to him by faith. These [Rom 7:7–25] are the words of a man set under the law and not yet under grace. He who is not yet under grace does not do the good he wills but the evil which he does not will, being overcome by concupiscence which derives its strength from the fact, not simply that he is mortal, but also that he is burdened by the weight of custom. . . .
>
> There is nothing easier for a man under the law than to will to do good and yet to do evil. He has no difficulty in willing, but it is not so easy to do what he wills. It is easy to do what he hates even against his will; just as a man thrown headlong has no difficulty in reaching the bottom, though he does not want to and indeed hates it. (ibid I.11–12)

The will, for Augustine, here, is "free" to choose *according to its reprobate desires*; but it naturally desires *evil* if it does not have grace. Without grace the will cannot cling to a true *good* in a way sufficient to realize a truly *meritorious* act, so irresistible are the parameters of

---

39. Here, we rely upon John H. S. Burleigh, trans., *Augustine: Earlier Writings*, (Philadelphia: The Westminster Press, 1953): 370–406. All quotations from Augustine's *Retractions*, II.1.i–ii and *De Diversis Quaestionibus* I, are taken from this source (370–371 and 372–406 respectively).

fallen nature. Grace *enables* the will to desire *good* with a *fullness*, thereby opening up for the will a *new arena* within which its inherent freedom could be exercised. Augustine's treatment of the issue here stresses that *grace* must *precede* any meritorious act of the will—even one's *initial stirring* of faith or repentance; for even if it comes by the *law*, the *law* is impressed upon us by God's grace.

Elsewhere, however, Augustine clearly takes human cooperation as a given, even as he stresses the absolute necessity of God's agency in grace. In his *De Continentia*, for instance, he speaks at length about this issue. There, using the metaphor of a soldier who is nourished, and who, thus, "by the help of the Lord wars down sin" (§ 7).[40] Augustine goes on, with exhortative, and emphatically *participatory* language, strongly suggestive of a doctrinal premise that, by God's grace, human beings *cooperate* with the Divine Agent in the project of our own personal salvation:

> Such soldiers the Apostolic trumpet enkindles for battle with that sound, "Therefore let not," saith he, "sin reign in your mortal body to obey its lusts; nor yield your members weapons of unrighteousness unto sin; but yield yourselves unto God, as living in place of dead, and your members weapons of righteousness unto God. . . . This, therefore, is the business in hand, so long as our mortal life under grace lasts, that sin, that is the lust of sin, . . . reign not in this our mortal body. But it is then shown to reign, if obedience be yielded to its desires. There is therefore in us lust of sin, which must not be suffered to reign; there are its desires which we must not obey, lest obeying it reign over us. (ibid. § 8)

As Augustine continues, his emphasis moves from that of *participatory agency* to *divine* agency, with the suggestion of human *passivity*. Accordingly, human beings are discussed as *instruments* to be taken up by supernatural enemies in the cosmic battle between God and Satan. He writes:

---

40. St. Augustine, *On Continence [De Continentia]*, Rev. C. L. Cornish, M.A., trans., in Philip Shaff, D.D., LL.D., ed., *A Select Library of Nicene and Post-Nicene Fathers of the Christian Church* (New York: Charles Scribner's Sons, 1917): vol. III, 377–393.

> Wherefore let not lust usurp our members, but let Continence claim them for herself; that they may be weapons of righteousness unto God, that they may not be weapons of unrighteousness unto sin; for thus sin shall not rule over us. For we are not under the Law, which indeed commandeth what is good yet giveth it not: but we are under Grace, which, making us to love that which the Law commands, is able to rule over the free. (ibid.)

At this point, Augustine again shifts his emphasis back to human agency and responsibility, *given the intervention of grace,* without which such agency is impossible. He writes:

> And also, when he exhorts us, that we live not after the flesh, lest we die, but that by the spirit we mortify the deeds of the flesh, that we may live; surely the trumpet which sounds, shows the war in which we are engaged, and enkindles us to contend keenly, and to do our enemies to death, that we be not done to death by them. . . . This is the acting of Continence: thus the works of the flesh are done to death. But they do to death those, whom falling away from Continence lust draweth into consent to do such works.
> But in order that we fall not away from Continence, we ought to watch specially against those snares of the suggestions of the devil, that we presume not of our own strength. (ibid. §§ 9–10)

According to this view, as Augustine articulates it here, human beings do, in fact, exercise agency in grace. That agency is of such a nature, furthermore, that not only can salvation be gained through our struggle, but also forfeited for the lack of it. While, indeed, we may once have enjoyed the supernatural power of grace, we can, nonetheless, abandon its influence, and along with it, our share in the life of the world to come.[41]

---

41. Of note, at this point in our discussion, is the fact that, here, at least, the thesis of *eternal security* finds no support. However much proponents of the thesis may look to Augustine as the definitive Patristic witness in its favor, Augustine himself clearly sees salvation, *this* side of the Judgment, as *forfeitable.* Indeed, Augustine makes this point, also, in his *Enchiridion* chs. 64–83, especially chs. 65 and 67. In 67, he references his book, *Of Faith and Work,* "in which," he says, "to the best of my ability, God assisting me, I have shown from scripture, that the faith which saves us is that which the Apostle Paul

Augustine's difficulty comes, however, in his inability to satisfactorily explain why some do not respond efficaciously to God's call, while others do. Returning to his *De Diversus Quaestionibus*, we read:

> Election does not precede justification, but follows it. No one is elected except he is different from him who is rejected. It is written that "God elected us before the foundation of the world" [Eph 1:4]. I do not see how this could be except by the way of foreknowledge. But here when he says, "Not of works but of him that calleth," he wants us to understand that it is not by election through merits, but by the free gift of God, so that no man may exult in his good works. "By the grace of God are we saved; and that not of ourselves; for it is the gift of God, not of works that no man should glory" [Eph. 2:8]. (II.6)

Augustine does seem to suggest a relationship between merit and election, but he insists that one must first be justified before one can "merit" in any meaningful sense of the term, such that strictly "meriting" one's salvation from good works is not possible, since salvation is given to the just, while one is justified not by good works, but by the intervention of God's grace. Still, for Augustine, the human being exercises some form of agency, even in the process of justification. He says, in Sermon 169:

> But God made you without you. You didn't, after all, give any consent to God making you. How were you to consent, if you didn't yet exist? So while he made you without you, he doesn't justify you without you. So he made you without your knowing it, he justifies you with your willing consent to it. Yet it's he that does the justifying. (§ 13)[42]

---

clearly enough describes when he says: 'For in Jesus Christ neither circumcision availeth anything, nor uncircumcision, but faith which worketh by love' [Eph 5:6]." See: St. Augustine, *The Enchiridion; or On Faith, Hope, and Love*, Professor J. F. Shaw, trans., in *A Select Library of Nicene and Post-Nicene Fathers*, vol. III, 229–276. For the citation above, see: vol. III, 259.

42. Saint Augustine, *Sermons (148–183)*, in John E. Rotelle, O.S.A., ed., *The Works of Saint Augustine: A Translation for the 21st Century*, Pt. III, Vol. 5, Edmund Hill, O.P., trans. (New Rochelle, New York: New City Press, 1992).

In the end, however, precisely how this dynamic unfolds—what happens as one responds to, or does not respond to, God's initial call—is left, by Augustine, in the realm of mystery. He is, thus, unable to give a systematic account of salvific grace which spares us from what must be seen, from a human vantage point, as a kind of sweepstakes of salvation. Though, we suggest, quite contrary to his clear intentions, Augustine sows, in the Church, the seeds of radical Predestinarianism.

For John Cassian, this shortcoming in Augustine is too serious to leave unaddressed. Cassian insists that human beings must be participants in their own salvation; and he contends that Augustine fails to allow, adequately, for this fact in his articulation of the relationship of grace to human choice. Unfortunately, Cassian places too strong an emphasis upon the dignity of the human will, leading him to an articulation which many regard as Semipelagian. This intellectual tug-of-war only serves to underscore the profundity of the paradox under consideration. A full reading of Cassian demonstrates with clarity that he is engaged in an earnest attempt to reconcile divine dependency with human free-will and merit, though he is, in the end, unable to do so in a way that fully captures the orthodox point of view. Cassian's struggle finds illustration in his Conferences. His difficulty there arises from his inability to imagine co-proximate causality, such as Aquinas will later introduce in his own attempt to deal with this paradox.

In Conference III, Cassian places upon the lips of Abbot Paphnutius, a response to the question posed by Germanus, "Where then is there room for free will, and how is it ascribed to our efforts that we are worthy of praise, if God both begins and ends everything in us which concerns our salvation?" (III.11).[43] Paphnutius discourses:

> This would fairly influence us, if in every work and practice, the beginning and the end were everything, and there were no middle in between. And so we know that God creates opportunities of salvation in various ways, it is in our power to

---

43. For relevant passages in Cassian's *Conferences*, we rely upon *The Conferences of John Cassian*, Part I, containing conferences I–X, in *The Works of John Cassian*, Rev. Edgar C. S. Gibson, M.A., trans., in Philip Schaff, D.D., LL.D. and Henry Wace, D.D., eds. *A Select Library of Nicene and Post-Nicene Fathers of the Christian Church*, Second Series, (vol. XI), (New York: The Christian Literature Company 1894), 291–409.

> make use of the opportunities granted to us by heaven more or less earnestly. For just as the offer came from God Who called him "get thee out of my country," so the obedience was on the part of Abraham who went forth; and as the fact that the saying "Come into the land" was carried into action, was the work of him who obeyed, so the addition of the words "which I will show thee" came from the grace of God Who commanded or promised it. But it is well for us to be sure that although we practice every virtue with unceasing efforts, yet with all our exertions and zeal we can never arrive at perfection, nor is mere human diligence and toil of itself sufficient to deserve to reach the splendid reward of bliss, unless we have secured it by means of the co-operation of the Lord, and His directing our heart to what is right. (III.12)

Because he does not understand co-proximity, Cassian is forced, in this passage, to present *God's* work as if it were sharply separated from *human* work. This is actually the same conceptual difficulty operative in Augustine's thesis[44] at *De Diversus Quaestionibus* II.2, where he dichotomizes between what *God* does and what *human beings* do saying:

> There are, therefore, inchoate beginnings of faith, which resemble conception. It is not enough to be conceived. A man must also be born if he is to attain to eternal life. None of these beginnings is without the grace of God's mercy. And good works, if there are any, *follow* and do not *precede* that grace.[45]

Augustine makes no distinction, here, between *metaphysical* or *absolute* priority and *temporal* priority, and thus, cannot offer a third alternative, namely, that good works may be simultaneous with the grace upon which they radically depend. In the absence of the concept

---

44. As we will see, this same conceptual difficulty is also at work in the thinking of the Protestant reformers, leading many of them to reject human power altogether, in favor of a hyper-Augustinian, *gnosticized* understanding of grace.

45. My *emphasis*.

of co-proximity, *Augustine* is led, as we have discussed, to emphasize human dependency upon grace in a way that ultimately diminishes human free-will and any meaningful sense of consequent responsibility. By contrast, *Cassian*, as in *Conferences* III.11–12, moves in the *opposite* direction in the face of this absence. For him, the emphasis is placed upon human free-will in a way that, at least when subjected to a *systematic* analysis, ultimately diminishes grace. As we have seen (*Conferences* III.12), for Cassian, God guides and exhorts human beings, while we struggle under our own power, receiving necessary *direction* and *encouragement* from God through *graced moments*. These come through Scripture, other Christians, the sacramental life, and the human conscience.[46] Augustine addresses precisely this sort of thesis in his work, *The Spirit and the Letter* (§ 4). There, he writes:

> But we must fiercely and strongly oppose those who think that the power of the human will can by itself, without the help of God, either attain righteousness or make progress in tending

---

46. Nonetheless, it would be wrong to suggest that a Semipelagian interpretation of Cassian is true to his *intentions*. Again, Cassian is attempting to preserve the dignity of human free-will and responsibility. He is not debating the necessity of grace *as such*. Illustrative of this point, and the fact that Cassian *does* grant, in some meaningful way, the salvific requirement of grace-through-faith, is Cassian's opposition to the Nestorians. Cassian sees Nestorianism as an *outgrowth* of Pelagianism, with which, he most certainly does not wish to be associated. For him, the view of Nestorius is tantamount to saying that the *mere human being*, Jesus of Nazareth, acted with a righteousness so profound, that, in his obediential act of baptism, he merited the indwelling of the Spirit to become the *Christ*. In his *On the Incarnation of the Lord*, Cassian discusses Matthew 16:13–20 as evidence in favor of an orthodox Christology, and maintains that no mere human being could *merit* salvific faith by his own powers (III.14). His further condemnation of the Nestorian position at III.13 underscores his claim that apart from a true faith in Christ given by grace, Cassian tells us, *there can be no merit* before God, and no human being can be saved. For a more thorough discussion of Cassian's involvement in the Pelagianism-Nestorianism-Augustinianism debate, see *The Works of John Cassian*, Rev. Edgar C. S. Gibson, M.A., trans., in Philip Schaff, D.D., LL.D. and Henry Wace, D.D., eds. *A Select Library of Nicene and Post-Nicene Fathers of the Christian Church*, Second Series, (vol. XI), (New York: The Christian Literature Company 1894), 190–193.

toward it. When these people begin to be pressed as to how they presume to claim that this is possible without God's help, they hold themselves in check and do not dare to make this claim, because they see that it is godless and intolerable. Rather, they say that these things are not done without God's help, because God created human beings with free choice and, by giving the commandments, he teaches them how they should live. Moreover, they say that he certainly helps them, insofar as by his teaching he removes ignorance so that human beings know what they should avoid and what they should pursue in their actions. Thus, by following the path pointed out to them, they may by the free choice implanted in their nature live chaste, righteous, and pious lives and merit to attain to the blessed and eternal life.[47]

For Augustine (ibid. § 5), the human free-will must be indwelled by the Holy Spirit in such a way that it instills in the human will a delight in the good things of God, and a desire to cling to his righteousness, not out of fear of punishment, but out of love for the Creator. He returns to this issue again (ibid. § 14), where he writes:

They say, "But we also praise God as the source of our justification inasmuch as he gave us the law so that, by considering it, we know how we ought to live." They do not listen to the words of scripture, *No flesh will be justified before God on the basis of the law* (Rom 3:20). It is, after all, possible [to be justified] before human beings, but not before him who sees the heart itself and the inner act of the will. There he sees what one would prefer to do, if it were permitted, even if one who fears the law does something else.

In the end, however, while Augustine sees human beings as real participants in the process of redemption, he *cannot* offer a clear

---

47. All quotations from Augustine's *The Spirit and the Letter* are taken from: Saint Augustine, *The Spirit and the Letter*, John E. Rotelle, O.S.A. ed., *The Works of Saint Augustine: A Translation for the 21st Century*, Part I, vol. 23, Roland J. Teske, S.J., trans. (Hyde Park, New York: New City Press, 1997): 139–202.

articulation of precisely *how* this participation occurs, given the fact of our radical dependency upon God, even for the *desire* to repent. A satisfactory resolution to the paradox must wait.

THE REFORMATION:
CALVINISM, LUTHERANISM, AND THE COUNCIL OF TRENT

It will suffice for us, here, to discuss the Reformation period under the representation of three groups—namely, Calvinism, Lutheranism, and Catholicism. Some readers will likely find this treatment too cursory, even given our purpose in the present volume. Because, however, the central issues of the faith-works controversy are so clearly defined in this episode of conflict, much of the relevant material, for our purposes, is dealt with elsewhere in the present volume. Our discussion in Chapter 1, for example, of the overall paradox, involves a treatment of Calvinism's internal struggle to deal with the question of human moral conduct within the life of grace. Thus, our presentation here is somewhat more broadly focused.

On the question central to this paradox, therefore, the Calvinists *reject* both human participation *and*, consequently, any discussion of merit before God. The Lutherans struggle to *affirm* some sense of human participation in the process of salvation, yet ultimately *reject* any notion of merit before God. Finally, Catholicism accepts *both* human participation, *and* some meaningful notion of merit before God.

While Lutheranism and Calvinism are fundamentally distinct in both their development and their theology, many of Luther's initial protests did frame the discussion within which Calvin ultimately took issue with Catholic teaching. For Luther, the notion that any act of penance or asceticism could *merit* the remission of just punishment due to sin in any respect was repugnant.[48] The very suggestion that a human being

---

48. One could argue quite plausibly that, in the end, all of Luther's objections to ecclesiastical authority, the weight of Tradition as a companion to Scripture, sacramental theology, and church discipline, are rooted in this issue. While we are not prepared to take up this discussion here, the reader is referred to *The Augsburg Confession*, where a line of thought can readily be traced through a comparison of the positions and arguments articulated in the follow-

could *merit* even *clemency*, seemed, to Luther and his followers, to undermine the notion of God's gratuitous activity in the process of redemption, and to trivialize the need for grace, or for fellowship with Christ. Still, classical Lutheranism, considered as a broader movement, did accept some notion of human participation in the salvific process, declaring in the *Formula of Concord* that, *after* conversion, a human being cooperates with grace (II.65–66). Nonetheless—and this represents a profound divergence from Catholic doctrine on the issue—the indwelling of the Holy Spirit is not itself the *cause* of our justification, since it occurs, according to the formulators, only *once we have been justified* (III.54) Thus, justification is not *intrinsic*, but is merely *imputed*—in a very limited, juridical sense—by a divine pardon, on the merit of Christ (III.22). For this reason, it is wholly meaningless, according to the Lutheran formulators, to discuss *merit* before God in any respect.

This difficulty on the part of the Lutheran formulators, of course, arises from an inability, shared with both Augustine and Cassian, to understand the notion of *co-proximity* with respect to causality. For the Lutherans, causality was understood in purely *sequential* terms, whereas within the Catholic tradition, especially as it is expressed in the work of Aquinas, causality can be both *simultaneous* and *co-proximate*, because God, who is always metaphysically *prior*, is an *extra-temporal* and *extra-spacial* agent, who can thus act outside a linear framework.

Calvin, however, again beginning with the same conceptual limitation with respect to the question of *co-proximity*, took this issue further, ultimately, than classical Lutheranism did. In the end, he affirmed, on the basis of his own reasoning, many of Luther's more radical personal theological assertions. That being said, we should remember that to treat Luther and Calvin fairly, we must understand each thinker's personal approach to the theological debate. Because Luther, who had been an Augustinian friar, tended, as did Augustine, to address issues, frequently, *as a respondent* to a perceived problem, his work does not lend itself, uniformly, to a precise systematic treatment, as would the work of Aquinas, for example. Luther's positions, therefore, cannot, in

---

ing chapters: II, IV–VI, XIII–XV, XVIII, XX, XXIV, XXVI–XXVIII. While this confession is not, of course, Luther's own work, it does reflect, we contend, many of his fundamental presuppositions.

many instances, fairly be taken as a definitive representation of his true mind on the subject. In many instances, we suggest, a more truthful summary of Luther's stance may be gained by turning to the work of the larger body of believers aligned with him; and that body, in the end, frequently affirmed a somewhat softer position than their master had articulated himself. With Calvin, however, the matter is different. He thought systematically and methodically; and his writings reflect the precision of thought he was accustomed to employing as a lawyer.

For Calvin, so certain was God's sovereign activity with respect to the redemption of the human person that any traditional notion of free-will could not be maintained. Of course, Calvin *did* accept the capacity of the human person to achieve, through the exercise of free-will, a kind of *moral* virtue, as opposed to properly *theological* virtue. That is to say that one could, according to Calvin, exercise free-choice, virtuously, in the *civic* arena, as far as that goes, but *not at all* in the arena of *grace*. His understanding of the matter precluded any sense, whatever, of human agency *in the assent into faith*; and to *this* extent, we say that for Calvin, the human person *lacks free-will*. At the precise moment, that is, when the issue of free-will assumes its true import as a metaphysical postulate, Calvin denies its operation altogether.

In the end, therefore, Calvin affirmed a "double-predestination" or *Predestinarianism*, wherein some human beings were predestined by God to be damned, while others were predestined to be saved (*Institutes* I.16–18). For Calvin, the pure gratuitousness of grace requires the denial of any real power within the human person to will or nill, except that power belonging to Christ. This power is *not*, in any sense, to be understood as a power belonging to the *redeemed*. He writes:

> If we no more bear fruit of ourselves than a branch buds out when it is plucked from the earth and deprived of moisture, we ought not to seek any further the potentiality of our nature for good. Nor is this conclusion doubtful: "Apart from me you can do nothing" [John 15:5]. He does not say that we are too weak to be sufficient unto ourselves, but in reducing us to nothing he excludes all estimation of even the slightest little ability. If grafted in Christ we bear fruit like a vine—which derives the energy for its growth from the moisture of the earth, from the dew of heaven, and from the quickening warmth of the sun—I see no share in good works remaining to us if we keep

unimpaired what is God's. (Ibid. II.3.ix)

It is clear, of course, that without Christ, and without the power of the indwelling of his Holy Spirit, we thoroughly lack any power of operation with respect to goods of a properly *supernatural* character, since it is precisely through *grace* and grace alone that we are *enabled* so to act. To *act* with respect to a supernatural good, that is, requires a supernatural *power of operation*—and that power is *supernatural* precisely inasmuch as it does *not* belong to us by virtue of our human nature alone. Calvin, however, goes much further, with this point, than the orthodox position requires; indeed, he goes further than the orthodox position *permits*. Calvin would be *correct* to say that, "we are too weak to be sufficient unto ourselves." He would be correct, and indeed, more precise, to say that this is not an issue of any strictly *quantitative* insufficiency at all, but one of the *qualitative* difference between the *finite* and the *infinite*, such that without God's agency in operation all the while, it is metaphysically impossible for us to love him. Calvin, however, is, in fact, *wrong*, from a Catholic point of view—and he is wrong, precisely for his failure to consider co-proximity—when he confesses, "I see no share in good works remaining to us if we keep unimpaired what is God's." Because he lacks the concept of co-proximity, Calvin is unable to conceive of a scenario in which God undergirds and empowers, not only human *activity*, but the very *agency* from which that activity is properly intuited by us to proceed. He thus, explicitly *rejects* the articulation, "we are too weak to be sufficient unto ourselves," insisting, instead, that we are *reduced to nothing* by the grace of Christ, such that we can claim no agency of our own at all.

Taking Paul's hyperbolic emphasis upon the power of redemption quite literally, therefore, Calvin claims that it is, indeed, Christ and *only Christ* who wills in the heart of the elect. The human will, wholly incapable of willing any true good, is destroyed, and literally *replaced* by the will of Christ—and all of this happens without any human cooperation (*Institutes* II.3.ix). As Paul proclaims, "I have been crucified with Christ; yet I live, no longer I, but Christ lives in me" (Gal 2:19–20a). For Calvin, then, the *irresistibility* and *total efficacy* of grace leads inevitably to the conclusion that by God's eternal predetermination, *some people are destined for damnation* because God, who chooses to save *one*, does not necessarily choose to save *this* one. Calvin cannot escape this conclusion. Indeed, he makes no attempt to escape it, but instead, affirms it emphatically. He writes:

> We do not, with the Stoics, contrive a necessity out of the perpetual connection and intimately related series of causes, which is contained in nature; but we make God the ruler and governor of all things, who in accordance with his wisdom has from the farthest limit of eternity decreed what he was going to do, and now by his might carries out what he has decreed. From this we declare that not only heaven and earth and the inanimate creatures, but also the plans and intentions of men, are so governed by his providence that they are borne by it straight to their appointed end. (Ibid. I.16.viii)

Calvin is clear. God *directs* the *intentions* of the human will, such that we intend *only* what God has foreordained for us to intend. If we are *saved*, it is because God has foreordained that we would accept him; if we are *damned*, it is because God has foreordained that we would reject him. In either case, these intentions are imposed upon us by God's eternal design for our lives, and for the universe itself. These inner intentions of will are, from eternity, borne, by God's direct agency, "straight to their appointed end"—that is, straight to heaven, or straight to hell.

These questions were finally taken up by the Council of Trent (A.D. 1545–1564), at the sixth session, from which was formulated the *Decree Concerning Justification* (January 13, 1547). There, the Council Fathers reaffirmed the Tradition of the Church regarding *intrinsic* justification through the indwelling of the Holy Spirit, and consequently, of the *merit* which flows from that indwelling. The Council affirmed that while justifying grace must be regarded as entirely *gratuitous*, it is still possible for the human person to *reject* that grace. God's prevenient activity *disposes* the human person to receive justification, *enabling* that person to *will God*; but it does not *compel* that choice. Nonetheless, because the power to *enter into intrinsic grace* is provided entirely by God, the human person's *actively willing* that choice is not, in itself, a *meritorious act*, but the *acceptance of an unmerited gift*. This gift, however, enables the human person to make *further* choices consistent with God's will, such that one's life of grace becomes meritorious *at the precise moment* the gift of that grace is accepted. That is to say that, because God's grace is now *intrinsic*, our choices and the actions which flow from them are now regarded as *meritorious*, even though they are continuously dependent upon God's undergirding, *enabling* grace.

Here, we ought to consider more closely the proper meaning of the term *imputed righteousness*, which is typically used in support of the claim of merely *forensic* justification, and, therefore, in contrast to the Catholic teaching of *intrinsic* justification. We suggest, however, that the term *imputed* righteousness, when most richly understood, does not, in fact, support the claim of *forensic justification* at all, but instead, better supports the claim of *intrinsic* justification. The problem lies in the fact that the term, *imputed righteousness*, has been used, in the past few hundred years, almost exclusively in its *juridical* sense, as meaning, *righteousness declared by the clemency of a judge (i.e. God)*. This understanding of the term, however, is by no means the only one valid. Etymologically, in fact, the term *imputation* implies something *internal*—i.e. an inner cleansing, settlement, or restoration. The suggestion, literally, is that *intrinsic justification* is precisely what God gives us when he *imputes* righteousness.[49] Thus, as the Fathers of the Council of Trent affirm, no human being is capable of self-glory, *regardless* of any capacity for merit, inasmuch as that capacity is granted us gratuitously by God, who goes on to sustain that capacity within us, through the indwelling of the Holy Spirit.

The *DE AUXILIIS* Controversy and its Aftermath

Conflict could be found, in the period surrounding the Reformation, even among Roman Catholic scholars, where the question of justifica-

---

49. Indeed, this view of imputation is consistent with Aquinas' understanding of God as the source and ultimate instantiation of truth (*Summa Contra Gentiles* I.60–62). Inasmuch as God is Truth-itself, he cannot tell a lie. From this perspective, therefore, the idea that the redeemed remain *totally depraved* in themselves, but are regarded by God *as if* they are righteous, is wholly incoherent, because it rests upon the absurd premise that God has assented to a lie. Thus, instead, we must recognize that while the phrase *imputed righteousness* has been used to *defend* the idea of merely *forensic* justification, the idea of *forensic* justification actually runs *counter* to the idea of *imputed righteousness* in its more essential, more traditional, and, we contend, more philosophically coherent sense.

tion was concerned. Roughly fifty years after Trent's sixth session issued its *Decree Concerning Justification* (January 15, 1547), Pope Clement VIII convened the *Congregatio de Auxiliis* (1598–1607) to deal with a dispute over the grace-freedom-merit dynamic, as it arose in the writings of Aquinas-commentators Luis de Molina (a Jesuit) and Domingo Báñez (a Dominican), respectively. In the end, the *de Auxiliis* controversy could, perhaps, blame its ultimate irresolution on a poor beginning. Consistent with Book I of Augustine's *De Diversus Quaestionibus*, Molina, in his *Concordia*[50], had looked to the mystery of *God's foreknowledge* for a resolution to the mystery of *efficacious grace*. This was a mistake for the obvious reason that the *former* is generally regarded as a more difficult problem than the *latter*. While the two issues are undoubtedly related at some level, one simply cannot escape the impracticality of attempting to resolve one through an appeal to the other. This impracticality nearly resulted in Molina's condemnation as a heretic.[51]

The *Báñezian* response to Molina, of course, suffered from its attempts to enter into this ill-framed discussion.[52] So impassable was the conceptual terrain of this discussion as laid-out by Molina, that after nine years and three popes, the debate was ordered silenced until further notice. That decision was reaffirmed by subsequent popes; and no final decision has been rendered to this day.

Molina attempts to show that God's knowledge can be understood

---

50. D. Ludovico Molina, *Concordia Liberi Arbitrii cum Gratiae Donis, Divina Præscientia, Providentia, Prædestinatione, et Reprobatione*, Sumtibus et Typis P. Lethielleux Editoris, (Parisiis: 1876).

51. A brief history of Molina's battle against condemnation can be found in T. Ryan, "Congregatio De Auxiliis," *The New Catholic Encyclopedia*, vol. IV, (Washington, DC: Catholic University of America, 1967): 168–171. *The New Catholic Encyclopedia* is hereafter referenced as NCE.

52. Our use of the term *Báñezian* is seen as incorrect according to W. J. Hill, "Báñez and Báñezianism," NCE, vol. II (58–50, especially 49). Hill claims that Báñez is Thomistic in every point. Cf., however, William R. O'Connor, "Molina and Bañez as Interpreters of St. Thomas Aquinas," *The New Scholasticism*, (XXI, 1947): 243–259. O'Connor defends, with strong textual support, the thesis that both Báñez and Molina fundamentally misrepresent the teaching of Aquinas on pivotal points relevant to the issue central to our study. See also, our nn. 53 and 55.

according to three modes. These are 1) his knowledge of *pure possibility*; 2) his knowledge of *free futures*; and 3) his knowledge of *absolute futures*. A *pure possibility* is something that God, by virtue of his absolute power, *could* create, but opts not to create in any time-frame.[53] *Absolute future* is a future which God preordains from eternity.[54] Molina's difficulty rests in his *third mode* of divine knowledge, however. He attempts to discern a *middle knowledge* (*scientia media*) between that of *pure possibility* and that of *absolute future*. Accordingly, God has knowledge of some realities that *could be*, but *need not be*, yet *will be in fact*. The problem, of course, is that Molina ultimately succeeds only in restating the paradox of *foreknowledge and human free-choice*. This, as we have said, is the wrong place to begin to look for a solution to the problem of grace and freedom. In the end, Molina must allow a moment at which God *takes his hands off* the creature and allows the creature to exercise power to actualize a possibility *without God's causal activity*. If Molina refrains from this implication, he cannot account for what makes God's knowledge of the consequent reality *middle*—if God ultimately and directly *causes* the reality, it cannot be called a merely *possible* future, but must be called an *absolute* future, since God's agency is *always* efficacious. In this way, Molina articulates a notion of *efficacious* grace which renders it only *accidentally* different from *sufficient* grace, the difference lying wholly in the *human response*. That is to say that, for Molina, the grace provided the human person by God is *identical* in the case of the one who is saved *and* in

---

53. Aquinas discusses this mode of divine knowledge at *Summa Theologiae* I.14.viii–ix, xi–xiii, xv–xvi. O'Connor points out (248–251) that Molina misinterprets Article ix when he treats that passage in his *Concordia*; and it seems that O'Connor is correct in his assessment. Aquinas understands God's *knowledge of vision* to behold those possibilities which will, in fact, never be in any time-frame. Precisely because God is eternal, and thus, simultaneously whole and utterly simple, his knowledge of possible and absolute futures are beheld in the same way. Contingency, therefore, has to do with the nature of the *object known*, not with the nature of the *knowledge* held. Thus, no *scientia media* (to be discussed momentarily in the body of our text) is actually called-for in Aquinas, because the *via media* resides, not in the eternal and unchanging God, but in the *creature* itself.

54. We will not attempt to discuss what futures fall into this category beyond, for example, that God would create the human race.

the case of the one who is not. The fact, then, that one is saved and the other is not must rest *entirely* upon *human agency*, and *not at all*, in the final analysis, upon any properly orthodox sense of *grace*, as such. There is no concept, within this framework, of a *co-proximate*, relational engagement with grace, such that one who attains salvation is enabled to attain it precisely under the *elevating power* of grace. Instead, it seems that, from this perspective, we step up to an ontological height, and then, in a wholly distinct moment, reach out entirely *on our own*. For this reason, Molina faced charges of Pelagianism.

The Báñezian reply to Molina, which the Dominican representatives at the *Congregatio* came to defend, seeks to address the obvious difficulties which arise in Molina's attempt to solve one paradox by appealing to another. Soon Báñez was accused of Lutheranism, and even Calvinism. This is because Báñez, continuing the discussion on the grounds of *foreknowledge*, must begin with the premise that God already knows infallibly who *will* be saved by his grace and who will *not* be saved.[55] Of course any truly orthodox theology must affirm such foreknowledge on God's part in a way that is meaningful; but, as we have said, this constitutes its own paradox—a paradox it is enormously disadvantageous to consider in a discussion of *grace*. If, as Báñez attempts to show, God's causal activity with respect to grace operates in a way quite parallel to his causal activity with respect to *nature*, the question of God's foreknowledge ought really to be considered as a problem having to do with the relationship between the *temporal* and the *atemporal*, while grace ought to be considered as a kind of creative activity on God's part.[56]

---

55. O'Connor (251–256) shows serious doctrinal divergence between Báñez and Aquinas with respect to the idea of *determination* as it relates to secondary causes and their effects. Báñez associates *determination* with the *contingent effect* while Aquinas associates *determination* with the *contingent nature of the secondary cause*. Báñez's teaching does not provide any adequate explanation for *contingency* in any meaningful sense. Aquinas' view, however, renders the idea of contingency not only *meaningful* but *understandable*. For Báñez himself, see Domingo Báñez, O.P., *Comentarios Inéditos a la Prima Secundae de Santo Tomás*, 3 vols. (Matriti, 1948).

56. Indeed, this *does* seem to be Aquinas' own approach. In his *Summa Theologiae* at I-II.109.i, Aquinas discusses divine causal activity with respect to nature and grace in precisely the same terms. This passage will be considered in Part II, Chapter 3 of our study.

Unfortunately, as we have said, Molina's approach changed the landscape upon which the discussion had been taking place to one that did not admit of a clear enough horizon for interlocutors to avoid the pitfalls before them. In attempting to avoid the difficulties of Molina's *middle way*, Báñez approached the paradox from the other direction. For him, the certainty of God's knowledge demanded that efficacious grace be *essentially* distinct from *sufficient* grace. That is because, if God already knows who will and will not be saved, and what God causes is utterly without defect, he must give grace either with the *intention* of its being *efficacious*, or else *not*. Paradoxically, however, this approach does not provide any definition of *sufficiency* still meaningful in light of divine foreknowledge. If *efficacious* grace alone is *truly* sufficient to bring the human person to salvation, *non-efficacious sufficient grace* is, actually, *insufficient* in the only respect that matters in the end. That is to say that grace, from Báñez's perspective, is only really *sufficient* if it is, in fact, *efficacious*. In his attempt, however, to account for human failure in the face of a gift of grace provided by an omnipotent, omniscient, and all-loving God, Báñez could not avoid this logical pitfall, try as he might. In the end, therefore, no adequate explanation could be given for the preservation of human *free-agency* within the context of grace, from within Báñez's framework. The so-called *physical pre-motion*—that is to say, the preparation for the reception of grace in the order of time and space—Báñez understood to be *given by God*. This *physical pre-motion*, however, was absolutely and exclusively *determinative* of the efficacy or inefficacy of the help God provided the human agent *through the actual offering of grace*. This meant that the human agent was, according to Báñez's model, in fact, either *enabled* or *not enabled* by God to attain salvation. As his critics pointed out when they called him a "Calvinist," this position suggested a kind of *Predestinarianism by election*, governed by a logic known only to God.

In the end, Pope Paul V, now the third pope to oversee the *Congregatio de Auxiliis*, closed the sessions of the *Congregatio* in 1607, without its scholars having arrived at a consensus. After nine years of heated debate, the pontiff brought the dispute to an indefinite end with the following words:

> In the matter of aids [*de auxiliis*] the right is granted by the Supreme Pontiff not only to the disputants but also to the

consultors of returning to their countries and homes; and it is added that this will be so that His Holiness may promulgate at an opportune time the declaration and conclusion which were awaited. But it was most seriously forbidden by the same Most Holy Lordship that in treating this question anyone either qualify the position opposite his own or note it with any censure. Even more he desires that they in turn abstain from harsh words indicating bitterness of mind.[57]

The scholarly community, however, could not so easily put aside this controversy. Even though, canonically, publication on the topic under discussion was made subject to the immediate discretion of the pope, this ordinance had only limited effect upon the scholarly dialogue. As Delumeau puts forth, pointedly, with respect to this matter, "Can one prevent men from asking whether they act or are acted on?"[58] In the aftermath of the *Congregatio de Auxiliis*, therefore, the scholarly community found itself still prone to further dispute on the topic at hand; and indeed, fears were gravely realized within roughly three decades after the close of sessions.

Cornelius Jansen would renew the controversy on grace and free-will, posthumously, with the publication of his *Augustinus* in 1640. He had written this compendium as a kind of *summa* of Augustinian thought. Within about thirteen years, on May 31, 1653, with his bull *Cum Occasione*, Pope Innocent X would go on to condemn five propositions associated with the *Augustinus*, all of which leaned heavily in the direction of Calvinism. Those who adhered to these tenets came to be known as "Jansenists."[59] Innocent had, in essence, condemned the

---

57. From the formula for ending disputes sent to the superior generals of the Order of Preachers and of the Society of Jesus, September 5, 1607. Henry Denzinger, *The Sources of Christian Dogma*, translated by Roy J. Deferrari from *Enchiridion Symbolorum*, 30th ed. (Binghamton, NY: B. Herder Book Co., 1957): #1090.

58. Jean Delumeau, *Catholicism between Luther and Voltaire: A New View of the Counter Reformation*, (Westminster: John Knox Press, 1977), 100.

59. For a brief introduction to Jansensim, see L. J. Cognet, "Jansenism," NCE, vol. VII, (Washington, DC: Catholic University of America, 1967): 820–824. See also, Delumeau's chapter on Jansenism in *Catholicism between Luther and Voltaire: A New View of the Counter Reformation*, 99–128. It is worthy of

Jansenists' acceptance of the claim of *limited atonement*, according to which Christ intends only to redeem those who, in fact, *attain* salvation in the *end*. This view relies upon a Predestinarian thesis which rests, again, in the problem of reconciling God's foreknowledge and omnipotence with human sinfulness, even in the face of the gospel.

If we wish to understand precisely where this particular problem rests, for the Jansenists, we must take account of a distinction. In Scholastic terminology, that is, we must draw a distinction between so-called *objective* redemption on the one hand, and *subjective* redemption on the other. *Objective* redemption is understood to mean, *the divine action of restoring an underlying fabric of justice in the cosmos through the death and resurrection of Christ*. Accordingly, Christ's sacrifice upon the Cross fundamentally reorders the cosmic balance in such a way as to constitute a kind of "new creation," or "renewal of creation," in the sense of *Revelation* 21:1–8, where Jesus says, "Behold, I make all things new" (v. 5). Christ's sacrifice on the Cross is seen as *objectively sufficient*, from an orthodox Catholic perspective, to bring salvation to *all* human beings. By contrast, *subjective* redemption is understood to mean, *the actual engagement of the individual with the divine action through the undergirding of God's enabling grace*, whereby God's grace becomes *actually efficacious* of *this* particular person's own salvation. In illustration of this distinction, we read, again in *Revelation*:

> Behold, I am coming soon. I bring with me the recompense I will give to each according to his deeds. I am the Alpha and the Omega, the first and the last, the beginning and the end.
>
> Blessed are they who wash their robes so as to have the right to the tree of life and enter the city through its gates. Outside are the dogs, the sorcerers, the unchaste, the murderers, the idol-worshipers, and all who love and practice deceit. (22:12–15)

Paul, likewise, draws this distinction when he says:

> [J]ust as through one transgression condemnation came upon all, so through one righteous act acquittal and life came to all. For just

---

note that Jansen himself, who had been bishop of Ypres in France (1636–1638), lived and died in communion with the Catholic Church.

as through the disobedience of one person the many were made sinners, so through the obedience of one the many will be made righteous. (Rom 5:18-19)

Thus, Paul is able to say elsewhere, "Now I rejoice in my sufferings for your sake, and in my flesh I am filling up what is lacking in the afflictions of Christ on behalf of his body, which is the church" (Col 1:24). For Paul, and for Catholicism, the afflictions of Christ lack *nothing* in terms of their *power* to bring about salvation; what Christ's afflictions lack is *not* power, but *our particular participation in them*.

For the Jansenists, as with the Calvinists, this distinction tends to be obscured. Because the will of an all-knowing, all-powerful God must *always* be efficacious, *Christ's* will to redeem can never be thwarted. Thus, in the absence of the distinction between *objective* and *subjective* redemption, grace is seen, by Jansenists and Calvinists alike, as *irresistible*; and Christ's death, therefore, is seen as redemptive *only for the predestined*. If we are *not* redeemed, it is because Christ does not *choose* to redeem us. Indeed, the fifth proposition condemned in *Cum Occasione* reads, "It is Semipelagian to say that Christ died or shed His blood for all men without exception."[60] As Innocent X understands them, the Jansenists equate the belief in Christ's universal sacrifice— that is, the claim of the *objective* redemption of the whole human race—with Semipelagianism. They say this because they suppose so-called *objective* redemption to be a sharply-divided momentary action on God's part, while so-called *subjective* redemption comes as a purely human response to what God *did* in the past. Again, this view fails to appreciate the orthodox position because it rests upon a more fundamental conceptual failure to understand the notion of *co-proximity*. God's action is seen as something done *in the past*, in contrast to our human response, which is seen as something done *subsequently* and *under our own natural efforts*. This view is false. Rather, Christ's redemptive action is *now* in the *eternal* order of things; and *our entrance* into the sacramental life of the Church is an entrance into *that* reality—an entrance enabled by, and undergirded by, God's *co-proximate* agency-in-grace. With the Janenist's conceptual failure on this point, therefore, they defend a thesis which returns them to the Báñezian difficulty according to which the only truly *sufficient* grace is

---

60. Denzinger, *The Sources of Christian Dogma*, #1096.

actually *efficacious* grace; and they must assert that we, as individuals, are either redeemed or not according to God's eternal decree.

As we will see, however, whatever the results of the *Congregatio de Auxiliis*, when we examine the intellectual landscape Aquinas lays outside his treatises on *foreknowledge, providence, predestination*, and the *Book of Life*, we find ground for alternatives to the pitfalls into which Báñez and Molina fall in their discussions of grace and free-will. We see, further, that we need not accept the hyper-Augustinian views embraced by the Calvinists and the Jansenists; for the issue *can* be, and *ought* to be, discussed from outside the context of the foreknowledge paradox. We propose, instead, that we turn with a fresh intellectual gaze at Aquinas' thought, and seek resolution to the problem of reconciling divine causality with human free-will and "merit" grounded in a nuanced understanding of the power of *theological virtue*. Theological virtue does, indeed, come to us through divine causation, but in fact, causes us to be *agents in our own right*, capable of responding to God in the "equality" of friendship. The idea of "merit", in any meaningful sense, depends upon this "equality" which comes to us *through* divine causation, as we will see. But how are we to understand the notion of *causality* in Aquinas' thinking such that this claim can make sense to us? How, in other words, can God *cause* "equality" between a creature and himself without destroying the very reality the creature brings to the encounter? How, that is, can we think *systematically* about what we have here termed *co-proximity*? We explore this question in detail in Part II of our study, where we find, in Aquinas' thought, a metaphysical apparatus particularly well-suited to this endeavor.

PART II

A Resolution of this Paradox in The Thought of St. Thomas Aquinas

Chapter 3

Aquinas on Causality in Nature and Grace

In this chapter, we will discuss the question of causality in nature and grace in the thought of St. Thomas Aquinas. Of central concern, therefore, will be the question of how God causes an elevation beyond a creature's natural capacities without destroying the nature of the being, and thus resulting in a substantial change. Our investigation into causality in nature and grace will proceed through three major points. These are: 1) The distinction between Aristotle and Aquinas on the four causes, 2) God as final and efficient cause of the human being, and 3) God as quasi-formal cause of the will in charity.

DISTINGUISHING BETWEEN ARISTOTLE AND AQUINAS ON THE FOUR CAUSES

Although it is frequently taken for granted that Aquinas adopts, wholesale, Aristotle's thinking on the question of four-fold causality, this assumption is simply inaccurate. We must bear in mind that since, in the classical sense, what we have come to refer to as "causes" should be understood more precisely as accounts of various dimensions of individual beings, the notion of a "cause" is intimately bound up with the ratio or the logos of a thing.[61] Thus, given Aquinas' disagreement with Aristotle concerning the nature of the creature's relationship to God, he simply cannot take Aristotle's treatment of causality as-is. For Aquinas, a truly Aristotelian understanding of causality is deficient by

---

61. This, of course, is among the central points at the heart of the prologue of John's Gospel. (1:1–18).

definition, because this relationship is not accurately taken into the accounting of the creature. Thus, how that relationship figures into each account or cause for Aquinas as distinct from Aristotle, is the central focus of this section of our discussion.

For Aristotle, God is an impersonal entity: conscious, and the source of all being, but still unconcerned about creation. Inasmuch as he is ultimate, there is, for Aristotle, no motive for God to contemplate anything beyond himself. The thought that thinks itself is always, already in completion. For Alexander of Aphrodisias, *De Anima* III.5 is to be understood in precisely this way. He writes:

> Since it thinks in actuality perpetually, it is itself exclusively intellect; it will therefore always be thinking itself. And exclusively [itself] in so far as it is simple; for intellect that is simple thinks a simple object and there is no other simple object of thought than itself. For this [intellect] is *unmixed* and immaterial and has nothing in itself in potentiality. It will therefore think itself exclusively. (*De Intellectu* 109.27-30)[62]

Aristotle writes, for his own part:

> And in fact thought, as we have described it, is what it is by virtue of becoming all things, while there is another which is what it is by virtue of making all things: this is a sort of positive state like light; for in a sense light makes potential colours into actual colours.
>
> Thought in this sense of it is inseparable, impassible, unmixed, since it is in its essential nature activity (for always the active is superior to the passive factor, the originating force to the matter).
>
> Actual knowledge is identical with its object: in the individual potential knowledge is in time prior to actual knowledge, but absolutely it is not prior even in time. It does not sometimes think and sometimes not think. When separated it is alone just what it

---

62. *The* De Intellectu *Attributed to Alexander of Aphrodisias*, in Frederic M. Schroeder and Robert B. Todd, trans., *Two Greek Aristotelian Commentators on the Intellect*, (Medieval Sources in Translation: 33, Toronto: Pontifical Institute of Medieval Studies, 1990).

is, and this alone is immortal and eternal . . . and without this nothing thinks. (*De Anima* III.5, 430ᵃ14–26)[63]

Aquinas' interpretation of this passage is radically different from that of Alexander. Aquinas interprets Aristotle to be speaking here of the immortality of the soul, arguing from the active power of the intellect, i.e. the *intellectus agens*, which Aquinas understands Aristotle to place inherently within each human soul. According to Alexander, however, Aristotle equates the agent intellect with *God*, making knowledge participatory rather than direct. This leads Aristotle to two positions, according to Alexander. First, the human soul is *not* immortal, since the principal of its agency is extrinsic. Secondly, and consequently, the *telos* of the human being is contemplation *within this life*, since contemplation must be, by definition, the *telos* of an animal that has *logos*, and, in the absence of personal immortality, there simply is no other way in which contemplation can occur. Thus, Aristotle's final causality is different from Aquinas', since Aquinas believes the human *telos* to consist in a friendship relationship with God: not just a participation in the divine mind, but an actualization of our intrinsic active powers.

This distinction is perhaps the most important point of contention between Aquinas and Aristotle (even if Aquinas did not notice it himself). For Aquinas, human beings are willed by God for our own sake. This is simply not so for Aristotle. While it is true that, for Aristotle, human beings value their own existence as an end in itself, and value their friends as ends in themselves, there is no metaphysical or cosmic correlate to this human valuing. For Aristotle, although our ontological *status* may be specifically distinct from that of any other kind of thing, human beings are the same as any other beings as far as our intrinsic ontological *value* is concerned. For Aquinas, however, all other being in the material world is ordered to the human person; we, ourselves, are the *telos* of the material universe, and are alone, among

---

63. Throughout the present work, we rely upon the translation by J. A. Smith in Jonathan Barnes, ed., *The Complete Works of Aristotle: The Revised Oxford Translation*, Vol. 1, (Bollingen Series LXXI • 2. Princeton: Princeton University Press, 1984), 641–692. The erroneous phrasing, "this *above* is immortal" which appears in Smith's translation as printed in the Barnes edition is corrected in our rendering, "this *alone* is immortal" (430ᵃ24).

material beings, ends in our own right.

 Where Aquinas and Aristotle agree, however, is in their belief that the human *telos* requires an end which is *other* than, that is to say *beyond*, ourselves. For Aristotle, according to Alexander, the agent intellect in which the passive intellect participates in human fulfillment, is *other than* human being. For Aquinas, while the agent intellect is *not* other than the human being, the *object* of which it lays hold (namely God) *is* other than the human being. The ultimate distinction, then, is this: for Aristotle, the possible intellect is actualized by being drawn up into the agent intellect, while for Aquinas, the possible intellect is actualized when the agent intellect is elevated by God, through grace, to a degree of power sufficient to the task of knowing him. That is to say that for Aristotle, the agent intellect is God, and it is God who does the real knowing, drawing us up into that activity, while for Aquinas, the agent intellect is *in each one of us individually*, and is *of* us. In both cases, the object in which the possible intellect finds fulfillment is God; but for Aristotle, the *only* real agent in the event is God himself, while for Aquinas, *God's* agency makes possible *human* agency.

 In other words, for Aquinas, while God makes human *agency* possible, for Aristotle, God only makes human *actuality* possible. The distinction here may be illustrated thusly: Fire makes possible both agency and simple actuality. While fire raises coal to the *actuality* of the *ember* for which the coal has the particular potentiality or δύναμις (*dynamis*), it simultaneously imparts to the now-actual *ember* a certain *agency*, i.e. the intrinsic *power* to emanate heat. By contrast, fire may make *iron* actually hot, but *not*, in itself, an *agent* of heat, capable of *producing heat from within itself.* The difficulty in this example, of course, cuts to the quick; for the process whereby the ember receives *agency* is the process whereby the *coal* is substantially altered. Aquinas does not maintain this parallel for human beings in the impartation of agency through *grace*. In *that* case, human beings are not so much made *something else* as made *something more*, in the sense of being made *more fully that which the substance as* this substance *can be*.

 This point brings us to the issue of *formal* causality. For Aquinas, we are, formally, intellectual *agents*, while for Aristotle, we are mere intellectual *actualities*. In either case, however, we have a paradox of significant proportions, indeed. How do we reconcile these two claims: God makes something actual, and God makes that same thing possible? The paradox is the same for both Aristotle and Aquinas. The distinction between the two figures on this point lies only in the *material object* toward which each understands the human being to be in motion. The resolution of this paradox, therefore (whichever thinker may be correct in the final analysis), lies in a proper understanding of *hylomorphic* theory. Too frequently the principles of *matter* and *form* are treated as ontologically distinct individuals which relate to the substance they constitute as parts relate to a whole. That view, however, misses the central thrust of the position, which understands matter and form as *dimensions of a single ontological whole* which they constitute through a set of so-called "real" relations.

At *Metaphysics* L.3 ($1069^b35-1070^a3$), Aristotle writes:

> Next we must observe that neither the matter nor the form comes to be—i.e. the proximate matter and form. For everything that changes *is* something and is changed *by* something *into* something. That *by which* it is changed is the primary mover; that which *is changed*, the matter; that *into which* it is changed, the form.[64]

Aquinas' interpretation of this passage is borne out in his *De Veritate* at XIV.5, where he writes:

> Whenever there are two moving principles or [moving] agents ordained to one-another, that which, in the effect, is from the superior agent is, as it were, formal, [and] what comes from the inferior agent is, as it were, material.[65]

In other words, the act of the lower being is potentiality for the higher being, such that the form of the lower is matter for the higher. Thus, by virtue of the *potency* of the higher being, the higher being can engage the *potentiality* within the *potentiality-actuality* relationship of the

---

64. My *emphasis*.

65. Quandocumquae enim sunt duo principia moventia vel agentia ad invicem ordinata, illud quod in effectu est ab agente superiori est sicut formale, quod vero est ab inferiori agente est sicut materiale.
The Latin is taken from, *Sancti Thomae de Aquino opera omnia* / jussu Leonis XIII P.M. edita ; cura et studio Fratrum praedicatorum. Thomus XXII, *Quaestiones disputatae de veritate*.

lower being, *through* the *actuality* within that being-constituting relationship. *Hylomorphism*, when precisely articulated, is not a kind of dualism as it is often caricatured, but a metaphysical *monism* rooted in a Platonic sensibility which Aristotle carries with him from the Academy.

Note Aquinas' interpretation of *Metaphysics* L.3 (at 1069^{b}35–1070^{a}4) in his *Commentary*. In this passage Aristotle says that neither matter nor form is generated; but clearly this cannot be taken to mean *all* matter and *all* form, since form exists in individuals who are generated, and matter exists in individuals who are generated (1069^{b}35). Instead, as Aquinas rightly sees it, Aristotle is discussing the two ends of the ontological spectrum, namely pure potentiality or *prime matter* on the one hand, and pure actuality or the *first mover* on the other:

> He says that "neither matter nor form [*species*] comes to be," or is generated.—But this must be understood to mean *ultimate* matter and *ultimate* form; for some matter *is* generated, namely the *subject of alteration*, for it is a composite substance.
>
> That neither *ultimate* form nor *ultimate* matter is generated he proves thusly. In all *change* there must be: a) some *subject* of change, which is *matter*; b) something *toward which* it is changed, which is *the moving-principle*; and c) something *into which* it is changed, which is the species and *form*. If, therefore, form *itself* and *pure* matter are generated, it follows that both form and matter have matter and form [themselves]. If [in other words,] not only *this whole* is generated—that is, *bronze sphere*—but also *sphericity* itself and *bronze* itself, an infinite regress in matters and forms [could result]. This is impossible. For this reason, it is necessary that there be a *stopping point* in generation—that, indeed, *ultimate* matter and *ultimate* form are *not* generated. (Lect. III.2442–2443)[66]

---

66. dicens quod materia nec "species fit," idest generatur.—Sed hoc intellegi oportet de ultima materia et de ultima forma. Nam materia aliqua generatur; scilicet quae est subjectum alterationis; est enim substantia composita.

Quod autem nec forma ultima nec materia ultima generentur, sic probat. In omni transmutatione oportet esse aliquid subjectum transmutationis, quod est materia, et aliquid a quo transmutatur, quod est principium movens, et aliquid in quod transmutatur, quod et species et forma. Si ergo ipsa forma et materia

Clearly, then, Aquinas' point, and Aristotle's, is not that *no* matter and *no* form has itself both a *material* and a *formal* dimension, but that there must be *some* matter and *some* form which are purely one or the other, namely *prime matter* and *pure actuality*.

The *hylomorphic* world is thus a world of *relations* between actual existents which manifest a spectrum of degrees of ontic power. An apple is actually an apple, but potentially a horse. That is to say that the actuality called "apple" is form with respect to itself, but matter with respect to a horse which can eat it. This is the point of Aristotle's discussion at *Metaphysics* Z.6, where he says that Socrates is the same as his form, and that this, i.e. the *form*, is the answer to the question *what is Socrates in respect of himself*, i.e. what is Socrates *actually*. Socrates is actually Socrates. It may, however, be asked, alternatively, *what is Socrates in respect of something else*, in which case the answer would be any number of things, for example, food for a lion—in other words, a lion. Thus, an actuality itself is at the same time a potentiality. The form is matter—not for itself, but for another. And the matter of another, in this case, *possible-horse*, is form in itself, i.e. *actual-apple*.

To restate the paradox currently under discussion, then, *how does God make an actuality possible*? Is it not *possibility* that is made *actual*? From what we have just said, we can already see the direction in which we must move to find our resolution. Aquinas confronts this issue implicitly at *Summa Theologiae* I.2.iii. The first way in which the existence of God can be proved, i.e. the argument from motion, and the third way, i.e. the argument from possibility and necessity, taken together, deal precisely with this issue: *making possible* through the juxtaposition of act, to which, through stages, being comes forth into higher and higher forms. This is Aquinas' philosophical illustration of Christianity's *exitus-reditus* dynamic which, in Bonaventure's thought, for example, can be worked out into a fully articulated theology of his-

---

generentur, puta si non solum generetur hoc totum, quod est aes rotundum, sed etia ipsa rotunditas, et ipsum aes, sequetur quod tam forma quam materia habeant materiam et formam, et sic ibitur infinitum in materiis et formis; quod est impossibile. Necesse est itaque stare in generatione, scilicet ultima forma et ultima materia non generetur.

The Latin is taken from, S. Thomae Aquinatis, *In Metaphysicam Aristotelis Commentaria*, (Taurini: Marietti, 1820).

tory.[67] In Aquinas' first way, accordingly, we see that a first and unmoved mover is necessary for there to be any reduction from potentiality to actuality. Then in the third way we see that in order for there to be any potentiality which can undergo a reduction in the first place, there must be something in itself necessary. This returns us to the point made in the first argument, that nothing can move from potentiality to actuality except by being brought into actuality by something already in act. That is to say that there can be no true potentiality without a corresponding actuality. An apple cannot be potentially horse unless there is already an actual horse to consume it and move it to a new act. The *actual* being makes *possibility* in another, and then renders that possibility actual through the *ontic power* of *agency* in the actual being. Thus, given the absurdity of an infinite regression of potentiality, we know that there must be a first moment of possibility, that is to say, of *ontic receptivity*, i.e. *prime matter*. Furthermore, we know that this fact rests in the prerequisite of something so actual in its own existence as to constitute the extrinsic possibility of everything else.

Aquinas' full argument, then, works this way: Because of the clear fact of *ontic receptivity* within the cosmos, and the absurdity of an infinite regression, we know that there must be at base, a *pure* condition of *ontic receptivity* as a perpetual *first moment* of cosmic being. That is to say, simply, that there is possibility at the root of all finite being. Further, because there can be no possibility at all in the absence of a *possibility-making* actuality to which it corresponds, we know that such a *possibility-making* actuality exists. And since the possibility at the root of all finite being is a *pure* possibility, it follows that the *possibility-making* actuality to which it corresponds is likewise a *pure* actuality, which has no possibility within itself, but is itself necessary, and causes all possibility outside itself; and this is what is meant by the term *God*. Thus, the ontological limits of all reality are established: at one end, *pure potentiality*, and at the other, *pure actuality*; but the former is itself made possible only by virtue of the latter.

We, therefore, see at this point, for Aquinas and Aristotle, three of the four causes illustrated sufficiently for the purposes of our discussion. Having arrived at an understanding of the authentic senses in which these causes are to be understood according to each thinker, we

---

67. See Joseph Ratzinger, *The Theology of History in St. Bonaventure*, trans. Zachary Hayes, O.F.M. (Chicago: Chicago University Press, 1971).

must take up the question of *efficient* causality. The central difference between Aristotle and Aquinas on this point is the question of *intention* on the part of the efficient cause.

It is true that for Aristotle there must be a first efficient cause which is outside the natural order, even though, as he understands it, the universe has always existed. The first efficient cause is not first *in time*, but first *metaphysically*. Aquinas and Aristotle hold the same opinion on this question up to this point. For Aristotle, however, because God is inherently fulfilled by virtue of his status as pure act, he lacks any motive for bringing other beings into existence. This does not mean that other beings do not come into existence *because* of him, but that bringing other beings into existence is not something he *intends* to do. He does not intend *not* to do it; he simply does not think about it. Since he is already totally self-sufficient, the first efficient cause lacks any *reason* to think about anything outside himself, and thus, simply does not do so. Because he already contains within himself everything there is to think, in other words, there simply *is* nothing else to think besides himself.

Admittedly, this line of reasoning is difficult for the Christian philosopher to counter. For Aquinas, the counter argument leaves Christianity with a paradox; for on the one hand, he maintains that God does not himself derive any further perfection from bringing other beings into existence. On the other hand, it is not possible for God to bring about an effect which is not fully and immediately present to the whole of his being—intellect and will. This is because God is not composed of distinct powers, but is simultaneously whole and simple. If God is causing something, therefore, he is *thinking* something and *willing* something, *ipso facto*. To put it simply, God does not have side-effects. A possible response to Aquinas' position, obviously, would be to say that God does not have a will, since he is already complete within himself. He has nothing to desire, no end yet to achieve, and so, no will. He is, in short, not capable of desire. This response, however, would fall short of the nuance of Aquinas' thinking on this subject. For Aquinas, God has a will which is in perpetual delectation. It does not *desire*, properly speaking, but it most certainly *intends*. We can and must say this, moreover, because *delection* is the *activity* of the will in the engagement of its object—the will as it is in its *fulfillment*. For the *hylomorphist*, we must recall, the true ontological starting-point is not mere *possibility*, but *actuality* and *fulfillment*. Since God, who is *pure* actuality is, *himself*, that ontological starting-point, his will must both *intend* and *delight*. God *intends* his object, and *delights* in that infallible act of intention.

Of the four causes as understood by both Aquinas and Aristotle, we can thus say the following:

1) An efficient cause is extrinsic to its effect.

2) A formal cause is the object itself considered as actual, i.e. in respect of itself.

3) A material cause is an object related to another object as potentiality to a corresponding actuality, such that a material cause is really a given object considered in respect of something *more actual than itself in some sense*, or else, in the case of *prime matter*, it is the very condition of pure possibility which arises as a result of pure actuality.

4) A final cause is a *possibility-making* actuality.

The differences between the two thinkers on each of these points are these:

1) With respect to the first efficient cause, Aristotle's does not *intend* to create while Aquinas' does.

2) With respect to the formal cause within human beings, the intellectual actuality of the human substance consists, for Aquinas, in our intrinsic intellectual *agency*, while for Aristotle, according to Alexander, it does not, but is merely derived from the intellectual agency of God.

3) With respect to material causality, Aristotle and Aquinas are in agreement, except inasmuch as Aquinas allows for the making of supra-natural possibilities where Aristotle does not.

4) For Aristotle, the ultimate final cause is never attained in any supra-natural way, but is found only in this life, while for Aquinas, precisely the opposite is to be affirmed: it is not attained in this life, but is attained only supra-naturally.

GOD AS FINAL AND EFFICIENT CAUSE OF THE HUMAN BEING

Having examined briefly what Aquinas understands by the various senses of causality in light of his conviction that God is a personal entity which cares about human beings, we must now turn our attention to exploring in greater depth the relationship between God's causative activity toward human beings in two respects, namely as our *efficient* cause and as our *final* cause. These two dimensions of God's causative activity will be examined together, rather than under separate headings, because they constitute a creative *dialectic* which cannot be properly illustrated otherwise.

As we have already said, Aquinas understands the ultimate fulfillment of human being to subsist in a relationship of friendship with God wherein God is present to the human mind. This is not, however, the whole character of human fulfillment. The intellect is not the sole power of the human person to be brought into actuality when a human being is ultimately fulfilled. On the contrary, the will and the intellect are essentially coequal in human fulfillment, just as they are throughout the kinetic continuum of human life. In this segment of our discussion, then, we will see how God causes both intellectual and volitional actualization in human beings, both *efficiently* and *finally*, while simultaneously preserving our nature and raising us above it.

As Aquinas says in *Summa Theologiae* I-II.10.iv, through divine providence, God:

> moves all things according to their condition, such that out of necessary causes, by way of the divine motion effects follow of necessity, but from contingent causes, effects follow contingently. Because, therefore, the will is an active principle, not determined to one thing, but being indifferent to many things, so God moves it that it is not determined to one thing out of necessity, but its movement remains contingent and not necessary, except with respect to those things by which it is moved naturally.[68]

---

68. omnia movet secundum eorum conditionem: ita quod ex causis necessariis per motionem divinam consequuntur effectus ex necessitate; ex causis autem contingentibus sequuntur effectus contingenter. Quia igitur voluntas est activum principium non determinatum ad unum, sed indifferenter

If we read this passage in light of the first two arguments for the existence of God in *Summa Theologiae* I.2.iii, it becomes very clear what is being said here concerning divine causality with respect to the created will. The first argument, the argument from *motion*, is distinct from the second argument, the argument from the nature of *efficient causality*, in that *motion* is a term associated principally with *final* causality in contrast to *efficient* causality. This is not to say that final causality *is* motion, but that final causality is the *ratio* of motion. Motion [*motus -ūs*], in its most rudimentary form is γένεσις (genesis)— that is, simple *coming-to-be*. As such, it is the fundamental characteristic of the material world. In its most noble form, however, it is the fundamental condition of any so-called "composite" substance: what Aristotle indicates by the use of the word κίνησις,[69] i.e. *the reduction of some specific potentiality to a corresponding specific actuality*. When the question is that of motion, *potentiality* must be understood as a *passivity* relative to some *active power*. Potentiality connotes an *ontic receptivity* which stands ready for being [*esse*].[70] In the case of κίνησις as such, we are, as we have said, speaking of a

---

se habens ad multa, sic Deus ipsam movet, quod non ex necessitate ad unum determinat, sed remanet motus eius contingens et non necessarius, nisi in his ad quae naturaliter movetur.

See also I-II.113.iii, which must be read in its entirety. Wherever *Summa Theologiae* is quoted in the present study, the Latin is taken from, S. Thomae Aquinatis Doctoris Angelici, Summa Theologiae, cum textu recensione Leonina, 4 vols., (Romae: Marietti, 1948).

69. For example, *Physics* $200^b12-231^a20$; $250^b11-267^b26$, and *Metaphysics* Z4 1029^b25; Z7, 9, 11, 16. See also Aquinas's *Commentary on Aristotle's Physics* and *Commentary on Aristotle's Metaphysics* on these texts, as well as *Summa Theologiae* I.5.i, where Aquinas discusses the identity of goodness with being according to desire and desirability, such that our very existence is bound up with desire, which desire implies *movement*.

70. For passages in Aquinas's texts in which the distinction between *active power* and *potentiality* are discussed, see *Summa Theologiae* I.25.i, where Aquinas says, "[P]otentia activa est principium agendi in aliud: potentia vero passiva est principium patiendi ab alio." That is, "*Active power* is the principle of agency over something else, whereas *passive power* (i.e. *potentiality*) is the principle of being acted upon by something else." See also *Summa Theologiae* I.25.iii.

specific potentiality—a *potentiality-for* a very definite type of being; and that *potentiality-for* must be understood, likewise, in relation to a *definite* actuality—i.e. *this specific kind of being*. This very *definite* direction, characteristic of κίνησις, is nothing other than *final causality*. It is a prerequisite for composite substance, or *substance-in-motion*. Indeed, since *all* matter, for Aquinas, is ordered to substantial being, even *movement-simply* (γένεσις) is subject to final causality, since, while not necessarily the movement of *substance*, it occurs within the material order *for the sake of* substance.

From within this paradigm, no matter what the impetus of any change (μεταβολή [*metabolei*]) or *motion*, it is always, at least in the grand scheme, *directional* and *specific* rather than *random* and *chaotic*. *Final* causality, therefore, is metaphysically prior to *all other modes* of causality within the created order. Thus, all other modes of causality, including *efficient* causality, must be understood with reference to a *final* cause. Where the interplay between *final* causality and other causal modes is especially rich, the *entire* dynamic may be described in terms of a *motion* rooted in the principle of *final* causality. Any understanding of that dynamic must rest in an understanding of the nature of the interplay between the *active power* of the agent or agents, and the *passive potentiality* of the patient or patients.

To understand this distinction properly, we must remember, as we have said, that for Aquinas, *final* causality is, quite literally, the *principal* mode[71] of causality in the cosmic order, with *efficient* causality coming second. With this premise in mind, it becomes clear that when efficient causality is discussed in terms of *motion*, the allusion is always to the *co-presence* of some *final* causality, without reference to which the efficient cause in question cannot be properly understood. That is to say that where efficient causality is discussed using the language of motion, it is discussed as a *facilitation* of that *motion* through which a specific *final cause* might be attained. The issue, then, when this sort of language is used, is less that of *making-to-be* or *doing-for*, and more that of *helping-to-become* or *helping-to-do*. To suggest that such a primacy of *final* causality renders God in any way impotent, is to rest in a modern scientific view of causality which sees only *efficient* cause as truly efficacious, and all other causal modes

---

71. Indeed, we may say not only the *principal* mode, but the *principle-mode*.

as merely analogously causative.

Aquinas's discussions concerning the automotive power of the intellect in *Summa Theologiae* I.79.ii–iii for example, provides a clear illustration of the interplay between *final* and *efficient* causality. On the one hand, the intellect is moved by the real being of the object to be known. On the other hand, the intellect engages the real object actively, which makes it possible for the object to move the intellect. In this sense, the intellect is said to move itself, i.e. by engaging the object of knowledge actively, in a sense, *seeking it out*. This manner of reducing something from potentiality to actuality involves *efficient causality*, even though the language is that of *motion*, which, as we have said, is primarily associated with *final* causality. The reason for this is that the active engagement by the intellect of the object of knowledge arises from within the intellect itself, by virtue of the intellect's own innate active power, that is by virtue of the *intellectus agens*. This is something the intellect is *doing on its own*. In that sense, we are, indeed, speaking of *efficient* causality—the *intellectus agens* is doing something within its environment, which ultimately leads to a gain in knowledge by the possible intellect. In this example, however, the intellect is faced with a *potentially intelligible object*, which it must *reduce* to *actual intelligibility*.[72] Thus, *final* causality, is *co-present* in this example:

1) The potentially intelligible object attracts the learner's attention, presenting itself to the intellectual appetite as *something to be known* (*final causality*).

2) The *intellectus agens* reaches out to the object by its own power (*efficient* causality), and . . .

3) draws the *potentially* intelligible object into *actual* intelligibility (*final* causality).

4) The *intelligible object*, is presented to the possible intellect by the *intellectus agens* (*efficient* causality); and . . .

---

72. The fact that the *potentially* intelligible object would come *prior* to *agency* in the intellect may seem a contradiction to the principle we have so far defended; but it is not. The object is *intelligible* only in *potentiality*, that very fact presupposes some *actuality* for the object *in its own right*—not *relative-to* something else, but *a se* or καθ' αὑτό.

5) the now *actually intelligible* object draws the *possible intellect* into a condition of *actual* apprehension (*final* causality).

Viewed from one perspective, therefore, the intellect moves itself as its own *efficient* cause, by virtue of its agent-power, the *intellectus agens*, which provides the intellect with a kind of *forward thrust* in the pursuit of knowledge. Conversely, however, the object *to be known* attracts the intellect *in the first place*, and moves the intellect *from without*, as its *final* cause.

As is the case with the intellect, the activity of the will involves a dialectic between *efficiency* and *finality*. In the case of the will, the object of desire presented to the will by the intellect moves the will from without, as its *final* cause (ibid. I-II.9.iv), while the will moves itself, as its own *efficient* cause, by its own internal act of willing the means by which the end is attained, i.e. by deciding to engage the object of desire actively.[73] In the movement of the will as in the movement of the intellect, *efficient* causality and *final* causality are *co-present*, since in both cases the agent *goes out* (*efficiency*) to an end (*finality*).

We must note, however, that in each of these cases, there remains an Agent *behind* the agent. In the order of metaphysical priority, the *first* final cause, and the *first* efficient cause of the creature's action, is God. His relationship of agency with respect to the free-creature, however, involves an activity of causation which is not only *compatible* with, but *creative of* the creature's *co-proximate* efficient causality of its own free acts. In *Summa Theologiae* I.105.v, Aquinas discusses God's causal activity as it operates in a world characterized by the creation of beings truly *other-than* God himself—beings whose acts of existence are *their own*, and who possess within themselves, their own powers of operation. He describes God's causal activity over such a world in terms of a hierarchical dialectic:

> Thus, then, God works in any worker whatsoever, according to these three [modes]. First indeed, [he works] according the order of the end. This is because every operation is [performed] on account of some good—true or apparent—and yet, nothing *is* [good] or *appears to be* good, except insofar as it participates in

---

73. See also I-II.10.ii.

a likeness to the highest Good, which is God. It follows [from this] that God himself is the cause of every operation, whatever it might be, as its end. Similarly also, [the point] must be considered that if several agents are set in order, the second always acts through the power of the first: for the first agent moves the second to agency. And because of this, all [things] act through the power of God himself; and therefore he is the cause of the action of every agent. Thirdly, [the point] must be considered that God not only moves things to operate, as if applying forms and powers to operation in the way that the *worker* applies the *axe* to split [wood]—who [though he *applies* the axe,] nevertheless, does not, *from moment-to-moment*, give *form* to the axe—but God gives *form* to created agents and *preserves them in being*. Thus, *not only* is he the cause of action by [*initially*] giving form, which is the principle of action—just as the generator is said to be the cause of the motion [of things] heavy and light [in the initial generative act]—but as himself *conserving* the forms and powers of things [*from moment-to-moment*], just as the *sun* is said to be the *cause* which enables colors to display themselves, inasmuch as it *gives and conserves light*, which[, as long as it is present,] facilitates the manifestation of colors.[74]

---

74. Sic igitur secundum haec tria Deus in quolibet operante operatur. Primo quidem, secundum rationem finis. Cum enim omnis operatio sit propter aliquod bonum verum vel apparens; nihil autem est vel apparet bonum, nisi secundum quod participat aliquam similitudinem summi boni, quod est Deus; sequitur quod ipse Deus sit cuiuslibet operationis causa ut finis. — Similiter etiam considerandum est quod, si sint multa agentia ordinata, semper secundum agens agit in virtute primi: nam primum agens movet secundum ad agendum. Et secundum hoc, omnia agunt in virtute ipsius Dei; et ita ipse est causa actionum omnium agentium. — Tertio, considerandum est quod Deus movet non solum res ad operandum, quasi applicando formas et virtutes rerum ad operationem, sicut etiam artifex applicat securim ad scindendum, qui tamen interdum formam securi non tribuit; sed etiam dat formam creaturis agentibus, et eas tenet in esse. Unde non solum est causa actionum inquantum dat formam quae est principium actionis, sicut generans dicitur esse causa motus gravium et levium; sed etiam sicut conservans formas et virtutes rerum; prout sol dicitur esse causa manifestationis colorum, inquantum dat et conservat lumen, quo manifestantur colores.

Aquinas addresses three points in this passage. First, all created being moves toward God—who is Pure Actuality—through the creative process of reduction from potentiality to actuality. Second, as possible-being is reduced to an actuality which it ultimately derives from God as *final* cause, it is *thrust* into created-being by God as the creature's *efficient* cause. The creature derives from the force of this act, the power to act upon something else. Finally, God's causative activity toward the creature is perpetual, and empowers the creature, not only for momentary *instrumental* action, but more importantly, for the *inner activity* of its proper operation as a being *in its own right*.

The dialectic described in this passage is paramount for our discussion. For Aquinas, the creature bears a likeness to God, because any movement from potential being to actual being is, by definition, a movement closer to God, who is Pure Actuality (ibid. I.2.iii).[75] By coming closer to God in this way, a being gains a higher measure of *active power*, because *active power* is the *power* inherent in the *act of being*.[76] In other words, God's pure actuality is synonymous with his absolute *active power*, or *omnipotence* (*Summa Theologiae* I.25.ii–iii). The creature, however, sustained in existence by God, has within itself, a degree of *active power* corresponding to the degree to which it is in act.[77] As *Summa Theologiae* I.105.v thus makes clear, the creature's *power* is its own, rooted in the very reality of *what the creature is*; but is *derived* from the power of God. This is because the creature's *act of existence*, though *its own*, arises only because God imposes being upon nothingness so what is *potential (on account of God's power)* might realize *actuality*. Thus, the individual acts which the creature performs are truly the *creature's acts*, because they proceed from the creature's own *active power*. Nonetheless, the creature is *entirely dependent* upon God for the performance of those acts, because the creature's *power*, by which it can act *in its own right*, itself derives from the God who *undergirds* the creature in the creature's *act of being*.

---

75. If the fourth way is read in light of the first way, it becomes clear that to be "more noble" is synonymous with being more fully in act. Thus, to be more like God is to be more fully in act, and conversely; and to be a higher substance is to be more fully in act, and thus, closer to the divine nature.

76. *Summa Theologiae* I.25.i, *Summa Contra Gentiles* II.7.iii.

77. *Summa Theologiae* I.25.ii–iii, *Summa Contra Gentiles* II.6.iv.

We see this at *Summa Theologiae* I-II.109.i, where Aquinas writes:

> Now every form bestowed upon created things by God has efficacy with respect to some determinate act, which it can [effect] according to its horizon of efficacy [*proprietatem*]. Beyond this [horizon], however, it [i.e. the created thing] can do nothing, except through some *superadded* form—water, for example, cannot *heat* unless *heated by* fire. And thus, the human intellect has *some* form, namely its own *intelligible light*, which of itself is sufficient for knowing certain intelligible [realities], namely, that is, that set of things-knowable [*notitiam*] we can arrive at through sensibility. To be sure, the human intellect cannot know [*cognoscere*] higher intelligibles, unless a stronger light complements it to a new fullness [*perficiatur*], as for example, the light of faith or of prophecy. This is called the *light of grace*, inasmuch as it is superadded to nature.
>
> Thus, it must be said that for the knowledge of any truth whatsoever, a human being needs divine help, so the intellect may be moved to its act by God. [A human being] does *not*, however, need a new inner-light [*illustratione*] *superadded to the natural* inner-light for the knowledge of truth in *all* [matters], but only in those certain things which *surpass his natural knowledge*. (I-II.109.i)[78]

Efficient causality, then, connotes an *energizing* (in the sense of the

---

78. Unaquaeque autem forma indita rebus creatis a Deo, habet efficaciam respectu alicuius actus determinati, in quem potest secundum suam proprietatem: ultra autem non potest nisi per aliquam formam superadditam, sicut aqua non potest aliquam formam, scilicet ipsum intelligibile lumen, quod est de se sufficiens ad calefacere nisi calefacta ab igne. Sic igitur intellectus humanus habet quaedam intelligibilia cognoscenda: ad ea scilicet in quorum notitiam per sensibilia possumus devenire. Altiora vero intelligibilia intellectus humanus cognoscere non potest nisi fortiori lumine perficiatur, sicut lumine fidei vel prophetiae; quod dicitur *lumen gratiae*, inquantum est naturae superadditum.

Sic igitur dicendum est quod ad cognitionem cuiuscumque veri, homo indiget auxilio divino ut intellectus a Deo moveatur ad suum actum. Non autem indiget ad cognoscendam veritatem in omnibus, nova illustratione superaddita naturali illustrationi; sed in quibusdam, quae exedunt naturalem cognitionem.

Greek ἐνέργεια [*energeia*], i.e. a *particular actuality*) or *making-to-be* (ποίησις [*poiesis*]), rather than an *allowing-to-become* or a *drawing-forth*, which is the work of *final* causality. While it is true, as we have said, that God acts toward us in both ways, we must understand the sense of that creative activity with respect to any given dimension of our being. We suggest accordingly, that *efficient* causality might be "softened" by *final* causality as the property of *innate active power* becomes more definitive of the kind of being that we are. In other words, as God creates a higher grade of being with a greater measure of innate power, the creature is, *as it is created to be*, more capable of contributing to its own action. Thus, God must do *less*, as the form he sustains in being can do *more*. Yet God remains—indeed, he is all the more—the creature's *final* cause; and thus, he acts, by proportion, more as an *end* or *motive* than as an *agent*. Again, this is not to say that God is *not* an agent, but that God's agency is directed toward the elevation and preservation of the *form*, which in turn, he makes capable of *acting on its own accord*.

What we see in ourselves as various *modes of being*, therefore, are the direct results of the manner of God's causative activity. In a sense, the mystery is misstated when we ask *how God's causality allows for the creation of truly self-determining being*. The appropriate way to state the mystery is to say that *self-determining being is what happens when God causes being in a certain way*. Thus, as we have said, contrary to God's causality being *incompatible* with our self-determinability, our self-determinability derives precisely *from* that specific mode of God's creative, causative activity which is "*making-human*."

One dimension of that creative activity involves the creation of the free-will, which is involved intimately with any properly *human* act (ibid. I-II.18–21); and the theological virtues are, though *infused*, properly *human* acts.[79] Certainly, in accordance with *Summa Theologiae*

---

79. While it might seem unusual to speak about a virtue, especially an infused virtue, as an *act*, this terminology is quite appropriate. A virtue implies a faculty functioning properly, i.e. fulfilled in its *telos*; and this is to be in act in that respect. Further, and more consistent with Aquinas' own usage, a theological virtue involves the will's movement, and that is for the will to elicit an act. The distinction here between the moral and the theological virtues on this point is that the moral virtues are operative habits inclining a person to a certain way of acting before a moral object in the created order, where a moral object may

I.2.iii, God is the first efficient cause of all things, which includes human-being and human-willing. Human-willing, however, is caused efficiently precisely *as free*; and God's causal activity with respect to our willing remains *freedom-producing* in the order of grace, just as in the order of nature. God's efficient causality with respect to the human will should thus be conceptualized in terms of the analogy of a therapist's supporting hand. Accordingly, the human will should be seen as the agent of its own action, but God as the agent who *facilitates* that action—the one upon whom the willing subject depends for the power of choice. For Aquinas, as *Summa Theologiae* I.105.v makes clear, this is an undeniable fact about the relationship of creature to Creator, both in the order of nature and in the order of grace. But precisely for that reason, the emphasis in his writings on the subject of human responsibility, even in the assent into faith, falls on the side of God's *final* causality with respect to the human will. As *efficient* cause, God makes human being with all that *"making-human"* implies, part of which is that we act of our own accord, without coercion, never being forced to will one object and not another (ibid. I-II.10.iv). But as *final* cause, God presents himself to us as *other*, and draws us forth to himself as an object of desire—an object which we may freely choose to pursue or not. God's *efficient* causality in this moment, which facilitates the will's power of choice for this *supra-natural* object (God himself), is sometimes called *enabling grace*. Enabling grace, however, does not, properly speaking, *move* the will, but *empowers* it for motion. As we have said, this is not because efficient causality is never discussed in terms of *motion*, but because when it is, the allusion is always to the co-presence of some *final* causality, without reference to which, the *efficient* causality under consideration cannot be properly understood.

Thus, if we understand divine causality with respect to the human will precisely under the aspect of *"making-human"*, we will understand

---

not always be present to elicit an act of the will. In the case of the theological virtues, however, the will's ultimate object is eternal and omnipresent, so that the inclination never ceases to culminate in an act of will, so long as the human being is conscious. The theological virtues, therefore, can be called *human* acts inasmuch as they represent the teleological fulfillment of those powers of the human being which constitute humanity's specific *differentia*, i.e. the intellect and the free-will, and subsist through charity in the willing of their ultimate *telos*: God himself.

God to:

1) cause *efficiently* in such a way as to give being to a creature to which God can . . .
2) present himself personally—as a *first supernatural final cause*—giving rise to a new, supernatural potentiality in the being . . .
3) which being will then be empowered by God, through the *co-presence* of God's *efficient* causality, with the ability to will this now-possible *telos*, in actual fact, though it is beyond unaided human nature . . .
4) in such a way that this creature can itself act as the *co-proximate* efficient cause of its own interior choice to engage God, while . . .
5) God draws this creature as the creature's consciously-chosen final cause.

As we can see then, free-choice, for Aquinas, does *not* suggest that human beings act *on their own* in their assent into faith, but that God causes that assent, both *efficiently* and *finally*, in the context of the creation-relationship whereby the self-determining being is sustained in existence.[80]

Let us examine this dialectic again. Human-being is created by God through an act of *efficient* causality *defined by an end*. The end by

---

80. See *Summa Theologiae* I.45.iii. Here Aquinas argues that while, in the act of creation, God does not move some pre-existent matter into being, but produces being without movement, creation is still something real for the creature, i.e. a *real relation* of the creature to the Creator—a relation according to which the creature derives its existence. The specific character of that relation, then, constitutes the very nature of the being, just as the character of real relations in the internal procession of the Trinity constitute the distinction of persons within the Godhead (*Summa Theologiae* I.28, 29.iv; *Compendium Theologiae* 52–56, 60). Thus, when we discuss the mode of God's creative activity with respect to the activity *"making-human"*, we are discussing the constitution of the specific character of the human creature's *real relation* to the Creator. How God causes us is what accounts for our species, because it is what accounts for the relation which constitutes that species.

which this act of efficient causality is defined, is the *final* cause: union with God in friendship. When God presents himself to a human being as a possible object of choice for a personal relationship, the human being is, in that moment, presented with a new possibility for actualization—one which reaches beyond the boundaries of the human being's own natural powers. This possibility, however, *remains unattainable* without some *elevation* of the human being's powers of operation. That elevation is caused, efficiently, by *enabling grace*. Now, while undergirding the creature's new *supernatural* power of operation for its new, *supernatural* end, God, as the *principal-agent*, facilitates the human agent's efficient causality of that creature's own act of free-choice. God does this, furthermore, *not* as a *remote* cause, but as a *co-proximate* empowering-efficient cause of the human being's choice. God does not *make* the choice; the creature does. Nor does God, in any respect, *coerce* the choice—for this would undermine the free-agency of the human will, removing from it the very character of its humanness. Rather, building upon the creature he has already been creating, God now makes of it *a creature that can make that choice*. The choice for (or, for that matter, in a *meaningful* way, *against*) friendship with God is *sustained* as a *possible actuality* for the creature by God's *continued self-disclosure*, as the creature chooses God consciously.

For this reason, in *Summa Theologiae* II-II.6.i, Aquinas names two requirements for the assent into faith, namely, the proposal of what is to be believed, and the assent itself. The first requirement can be met either by divine illumination, or else, and ordinarily, in the form of a preacher's exhortation. The second requirement must be considered in light of a causal dynamic, which we have endeavored to treat thus far in the present chapter. Here, Aquinas draws a distinction between two modes of causality which support the interpretation we have given to the other texts we have considered:

> One, indeed, draws from without, for example, witnessing a miracle, or human persuasion soliciting unto belief. None, however, is a sufficient cause; for one and the same miracle has been seen, and the same proclamation heard, yet one believes and another does not believe. It is, therefore, essential that we affirm another, *interior* cause, which moves the human being inwardly to assent to the things of faith. Now, this cause the Pelagians thought to be human free-will alone and therefore said that the

initiation of faith is from us, evidently saying that it is from the ground of ourselves that we are prepared to assent to the things of faith; but the consummation of faith is from God, i.e. that he goes on to propose things which we are then bound to believe. But this is false. This is because a human being, in assenting to the things of faith, is raised above his nature, he has this assent from a supernatural principle moving him from within, which [principle] is God. The assent of faith, therefore, which is the principal act of faith, is from God moving us inwardly through grace.[81]

O'Brien[82] sees this passage as suggesting *efficient* causality on the part of God in the assent of the human being into faith. We have already acknowledged that God *does* act toward us, in this moment, as *first* and *co-proximate* efficient cause, and that in the assent into faith, the human will is the *secondary co-proximate* efficient cause of its own activity. Thus, of course, we maintain that God's efficient causality in the assent into faith is not wholly absent. Indeed, we are "raised above our nature" by a divine act of efficient causality—an efficient causality by which our choice for faith is *facilitated*—an efficient causality whereby we are *enabled* to choose for it, by a new active power of our own. Nevertheless, we cannot maintain that God causes even this

---

81. Una quidem exterius inducens: sicut miraculum visum, vel persuasio hominis inducentis ad fidem. Quorum neutrum est sufficiens causa: videntium enim unum et idem miraculum, et audientium eandem praedicationem, quidam credunt et quidam non credunt. Et ideo oportet ponere aliam causam interiorem, quae movet hominem interius ad assentiendum his quae sunt fidei. Hanc autem causam Pelagiani ponebant solum liberum arbitrium hominis: et propter hoc dicebant quod initium fidei est ex nobis, inquantum scilicet ex nobis est quod parati sumus ad assentiendum his quae sunt fidei; sed consummatio fidei est a Deo, per quem [Piana reads *quam*] nobis proponuntur ea quae credere debemus. Sed hoc est falsum. Quia cum homo assentiendo his quae sunt fidei, elevetur supra naturam suam, oportet quod hoc insit ei ex supernaturali principio interius movente, quod est Deus. Et ideo fides quantum ad assensum [Piana reads *assentiendum*], qui est principalis actus fidei, est a Deo interius movente per gratiam.

82. O'Brien, 167 note g in *Summa Theologiae*. (Vol. 31). T. C. O'Brien, trans., (New York, McGraw-Hill Book Company, 1974).

supernatural act of assent *efficiently* in such a way as to deny, or render meaningless, the real, if only *co-proximate*, efficient causality elicited by the will itself. Aquinas himself insists upon this, as we have seen, in I-II.10.iv, and will again in II-II.23.ii, which we will examine later. O'Brien is certainly right in seeing *efficient* causality at work here in the way we have discussed it, i.e. as *enabling grace*. Nonetheless, the discussion suggests also, and perhaps more primarily (and in keeping with Aquinas' comments in other passages) *final causality* of a sort similar to that discussed in I.2.iii, in the argument from motion. There, God is seen to bring about by an act of will an *ontic receptivity* where before there had been nothing. This is then drawn toward him as pure possibility to pure actuality—a movement of creation brought about by God, which God then answers with the efficient causation of particular being. The receptivity for particular being (*prime matter*) is brought about by God, to whom it relates as to its final cause. In the same way, the *ontic receptivity* for theological virtue is brought about by God in an act of creation over and above our natural coming-to-be; and we relate to him as to our final cause. Thus, II-II.2.ix ad 3 describes as a "sufficient solicitation to belief" [*sufficiens inductivum ad credendum*] the "interior excitement of God inviting us" [*interiori instinctu Dei invitantis*].[83] Again, the language is clearly that of *final* causality. In this way, we can see the infusion of the theological virtues as an act of creation concerning the human person, and caused according to the condition of human being:

> such that out of necessary causes, by way of the divine motion effects follow of necessity, but from contingent causes, effects follow contingently. . . . [and] the will is not determined to one thing out of necessity, but its movement remains contingent and

---

83. O'Brien translates *sufficiens inductivum ad credendum* as "a sufficient motive for believing." This rendering is consistent with his understanding of the *interiori instinctu* as suggesting *efficient* causality (see pp. 98–99 note i, and 167 note g). While this rendering under-emphasizes the *co-presence* of *final* causality in this moment, his translation of *interiori instinctu Dei invitantis* as "the inner inspiration of God inviting him to believe" still reflects the sense of *final* causality shared by the word *inductivum*: "a solicitation" or "a drawing force," from *indūco -dūc re -duxi -ductum*: "to lead in." See also n. 85 in this study.

not necessary. (ibid. I-II.10.iv)

Returning, then, to the text at *Summa Theologiae* II-II.2.iii, where Aquinas discusses the will as being unable "to *stretch out [pertingere]* to the vision of God except by way of learning from God as from a teacher," we see how profoundly *interactive*, for Aquinas, is the assent of the human person into the life of faith. The imagery employed by Aquinas in this passage calls upon the classical understanding of the *educative process*, a phrase wherein both terms are key. We speak of a *process* in the sense of the Greek κίνησις as previously discussed in this chapter, namely as a *movement-toward* some end. We speak of this process as *educative* in the sense of the Latin *educare*, i.e. *to lead out*. Thus, we speak about faith in Aquinas' thought, as a process whereby one is *led out* of the darkness of ignorance by God, through charity, ultimately into the light of glory, the Beatific Vision.

The educative process includes not just an escape from *ignorance* considered as a condition of the intellect, but an escape from the inward-turning of the will, and thus, a *leading out* from the Self to embrace God and the whole communion of saints, whereby the faithful person becomes incorporated into the Church and an heir in the kingdom of heaven.[84] This is why charity is said, by Aquinas, to be the full-

---

84. Incorporation into a larger community as the social term of the educative process is common to classical thought. For Aquinas, as for Aristotle, the epistemological position of "moderate realism" presumes a world external to the knower, but not *removed*. The world is *about* us, and we are part of it; and we come to commune with other being consciously through our intellectual faculties. Thus, the more fully those powers are actualized the more thoroughly we enter into communion with other being—a process which, for Aquinas, culminates in communion with *subsistent being [ipsum esse subsistens]*, i.e. God.

In the Platonic corpus, we are drawn to consider especially the allegory of the cave, which brings out vividly the imagery later employed by Aquinas. Plato tellingly places this discussion in the heart of his *Republic* (VII), wherein he considers the various directions in which the human community can move as a *polis*. In this allegory, a group of prisoners are bound by their own private imaginings—imaginings which may be called *private* in the most literal sense of the term, i.e. *lacking some due form*. These prisoners are unable to escape their *privative* condition without the aid of one already enlightened, and are drawn by the *free* person into the light of day, *above ground* to the human community, where, we are to presume, they are incorporated as citizens of the

form of faith (ibid. II-II.2.ix *ad* 1), what Aristotle would have called faith's ἐντελέχεια (*entelecheia*). It implies not only the intellect, but also the will moving out toward God.[85] It is impossible to consider the act of faith without reference to its final form in charity, which gives shape and meaning to faith's intellectual assent (ibid. II-II.2.ix *ad* 1). As we have already seen, faith is an intellectual assent made by an act of the grace-enabled will as it is drawn forth by God. Charity, on the other hand, is an act of the grace-enabled will whereby the human person cleaves to God as apprehended through faith. Inasmuch as charity is faith's final form, it must be analyzed in the same way as faith. Aquinas' treatment of causality in the theological virtue of charity bares this out, and is explicit in laying out the parameters of the orthodox position as he understands it:

> Indeed, the movement of charity does *not* proceed from the Holy Spirit moving the human mind such that the mind is but *moved*, in no way being the *principle* of this [motion], as when some *body* is moved by some exterior mover. This [way of thinking],

---

republic. While Plato uses this allegory to depict the solitary journey of the philosopher through life, he certainly implies that it is only by making such a journey that true community becomes possible. Ignorance imprisons us, and actually isolates us from the rest of the world, and from our fellow human beings. For those in the cave, even their awareness of their fellow prisoners is a vague and "shadowy" one at best. Aquinas, like Plato, sees education as fundamental to the political question, only for Aquinas, the *polis*—the human community—is to be drawn up as Church into the kingdom of heaven.

An interesting remnant of this classical theory of education as *incorporative* into the *public realm* is seen in military ranking. Therein, the rank of *private* is lowest and without authority, while *corporal* denotes a degree of completion. The *corporal* is no longer on the outer fringe of military life, but on account of experience and training is drawn into the *body*, i.e. the *corps*.

85. We have already discussed the integration of the will and the intellect in the assent into faith. In this sense, the mention of charity gives us nothing new. What we wish to suggest, however, is that the consideration of the theological virtue of charity as the full form of faith completes the integration we have already discussed. While by the assent of faith the will moves the intellect to belief, in charity, the will moves itself toward that which is presented to it by the intellect which "*stretches out*" toward its object (God) through faith, even as that movement is sustained by God's grace.

indeed, is contrary to the [very] *ratio* of a voluntary [act], the principle of which must be *within itself*, as stated above (I-II.6.i). It therefore follows [from such a stance] that to love is *not voluntary*. This implies a contradiction, since love, *of its very nature*, is an *act of the will*.

Similarly, it can neither be said that the Holy Spirit moves the will to an act of love as if moving an *instrument*, which is, granted, a principle of action, but is not of *itself* [empowered] to act or not to act. Thus again, indeed, [from within such a framework,] the *ratio* of the voluntary is destroyed, and the *ratio* of merit is excluded. Yet, above it is maintained (I-II.114.iv) that the love of charity is the *root of merit*. It must be, then, that the Holy Spirit so moves the will to [the act] of love that [even as it is being moved,] it remains the efficient cause of its own act. (Ibid. II-II.23.ii)[86]

As this passage makes clear, Aquinas maintains that God causes theological virtue in us in such a way as to make it truly *our* activity, yet it remains radically dependent upon his special activity of creation called "grace," by which an existing creature is made capable of reaching beyond the powers of its own nature, without ceasing to be what it is. In this case, what we are is *self-determining being*; thus grace, if it is truly *grace*, must operate *in the context* of our free-will, so that the *supra-natural* activity which it makes possible does not annihilate us, but takes us up into the divine life.

---

86. Non enim motus caritatis ita procedit a Spiritu Sancto movente humanam mentem quod humana mens sit mota tantum et nullo modo sit principium huius motus, sicut cum aliquod corpus movetur ab aliquo exteriori movente. Hoc enim est contra rationem voluntarii, cuius oportet principium in ipso esse, sicut supra dictum est. Unde sequeretur quod diligere non esset voluntarium. Quod implicat contradictionem: cum amor de sui ratione importet quod sit actus voluntatis.—Similiter etiam non potest dici quod sic moveat Spiritus Sanctus voluntatem ad actum diligendi sicut movetur instrumentum, quod esti sit principium actus, non tamen est in ipso agere vel non agere. Sic enim etiam tolleretur ratio voluntarii, et excluderetur ratio meriti: cum tamen supra habitum sit quod dilectio caritatis est radix merendi.—Sed oportet quod sic voluntas moveatur a Spiritu Sancto ad diligendum quod etiam ipsa sit efficiens hunc actum.

God as Quasi-Formal Cause of the Will in Charity

The creative activity whereby God perfects the human will in the theological virtue of charity is perhaps the most paradoxical, or at least the most mystical mode of creative activity which he directs toward human being. It may be referred to as a kind of *quasi-formal* causation, whereby God himself comes to reside in the human will, not so as to come into composition with it, which would be absurd, but so as to *fulfill its operation*. This issue arises, for Aquinas, within the context of the question of *merit* before God with respect to the rewards of salvation. Aquinas argues that in fact, merit is possible before God, even though by nature we lack any equality with God from which merit could be claimed. His position rests upon the affirmation that equality with God, at least *analogously* speaking, can, in fact, be attained by human beings *through grace*. In this case, the grace in question is *God's self-gift* to the human person through the forgiveness of sins, whereby we are restored by God to a friendship relationship with him. When this relationship is established by God's prerogative as a fulfillment of the *movement-toward* God which he enables, the Holy Spirit enters into the human soul and dwells there, fulfilling the human will's movement. Once again, we see God standing over-against us as a *possibility-making* actuality, and then reducing that possibility to which he has given rise in us, to *actuality*. As we discussed in the first segment of this chapter, however, when we speak of a particular actuality which stands as the direct fulfillment of some specific potentiality, we are speaking of none other than the *form* of the thing—the thing considered as *actual*. In the case, however, of the will fulfilled in charity by the "indwelling" of the Holy Spirit, we simply cannot say in an unqualified sense that we are speaking properly of the will's *formal* character. This is because the Holy Spirit which fulfills the will remains *truly distinct* from the will, even as it unites itself intimately with the will. In any case, because of this *intimacy* between the Holy Spirit and the will it "indwells," we *are* speaking of something *like* the will's formal character (Ibid. II-II.2.ix ad 1). Precisely how this mystery is to be understood, however, requires discussion.

There is a sense in which the will *becomes* the object toward which it *stretches out*, just as the intellect in a sense *becomes* the object known. The will lays hold of its object just as the mind does. In the case of theological virtue by which one possesses a *habitus* toward God himself, there is a sense in which the will *becomes* God, its proper object, the ultimate *final cause* of the activity called the *life of faith*. It is God who enables the will so to *stretch out*, and it is God himself who fulfills the will, making himself present to it in a personal way. This is *not* to say that God enters into *composition* with the human person, but that he perfects the *being-in-relation* for which all human beings are designed,[87] allowing the human person to enter into friendship with him (II-II.23.iii). The will "becomes" God in the same sense that it becomes any beloved person it beholds; but in the case of theological virtue, the possession of God by the will, made possible in the human person by God's own power, and being the *ultimate* relational *terminus* of the human person, brings *ultimate* fulfillment to the human person, who *comes-to-be* by virtue of, and *directed-toward* relationality.[88] Though not our substance, our world of inter-relations is nonetheless *bound-up with* the fulfillment of our substance; that is to say, it is ontologically linked to our process of becoming what we are—our κίνησις. It is in this sense that we say that our will *becomes* the object it beholds. The beholding of that object is the *telos* of the will's act. To have the object of desire present to the willing person, is for the will of that person to be most fully in act. Thus, the presence of God in the human will is the will's most perfect actuality.

The crucial text to be considered on this point is *Summa Theologiae* II-II.23.ii, to which reference was made earlier. Here, Aquinas asks *whether charity is anything created in the soul*. In answering this question, Aquinas draws a distinction between what imbues charity with its power and charity itself considered as a *movement-toward* God. The latter, says Aquinas, i.e. charity itself, is indeed something creaturely in the soul, since it is the soul's own movement—the activity of the soul itself, which is creaturely. But what imbues this movement with its power is God himself, in the person of the Holy Spirit who dwells in

---

87. For a fuller discussion of this issue, see W. Norris Clarke, S.J. *Person and Being*. ([The Aquinas Lecture, 1993] Milwaukee: Marquette University Press, 1993).

88. We here recall *Summa Theologiae* II-II.2.iv, where Aquinas speaks of a person standing with a relation-toward God [*relatus in Deum*]. See again nn. 79, 80, and 90 in this study.

the soul now bound to him in friendship. Thus in *ad* 1, Aquinas writes:

> The divine essence itself is charity, just as it is wisdom, and just as it is goodness. Now we are said to be good with the goodness which is God, and wise with the wisdom which is God, because the goodness which makes us formally good is a participation in the divine goodness; and the wisdom which makes us formally wise is a participation in the divine wisdom. So, too, the charity by which we formally love those about us is a participation in the divine charity.[89]

As discussed earlier, grace is a special creative act on God's part, which adds to a creature some degree of perfection over and above what is intrinsic to it through its natural powers—i.e. it is some *supranatural* act of creation which elevates the being of the creature who receives it, yet without the creature's destruction—that is, without a substantial change.

---

89. [I]psa essentia divina caritas est, sicut et sapientia est, et sicut bonitas est. Unde sicut dicimur boni bonitate quae Deus est, et sapientes sapientia quae Deus est, quia bonitas qua formaliter boni sumus est participatio quaedam divinae bonitatis, et sapientia qua formaliter sapientes sumus est participatio quaedam divinae sapientiae; ita etiam caritas qua formaliter diligimus proximum est quaedam participatio divinae caritatis.

Chapter 4

Aquinas on Merit in Nature and Grace

Having discussed the various senses of causality in the will with respect to theological virtue, we must now consider the meaning of the claim of "merit" in that light. In this chapter, therefore, we more thoroughly examine the idea of "merit," asking how it is to be understood, according to Aquinas, and what its parameters are within the context of theological virtue. As we discussed in the preceding chapter, Aquinas understands *charity*, i.e. the *indwelling of the Holy Spirit*, to cause an *elevation* of the power of the human will for *agency beyond our natural ability*. It is, therefore, as we will see, the root of all true *merit* before God.

Charity, however, is, in its fundamental character, an *interpersonal relationship*, and is *understood as such* by Aquinas. In the relation of friendship whereby we are joined to God, God *resides* in the will and perfects it, i.e. completes it, *raising it to a new fullness*. The relation of friendship with God, which completes theological virtue, is a quality of the human subject caused in us *efficiently* by our own free choice working with grace, but *finally* by God who draws us, and *formally* by God who resides in our will once we are raised to charity. It is on this basis that Aquinas can say at I-II.114.iv that grace is the principle of merit, which comes through charity. On the other hand, precisely *because* charity is an interpersonal relationship, *what* we can merit through grace is determined by the *character* of that relationship.

In the passage at II-II.23.ii, Aquinas asserts that a claim of merit depends upon the assent into faith being freely made, and emerging from within the power of the human will. The language here, as in I-II.10.iv, is that of *final* causality on God's part. In *Summa Theologiae* II-II.2.ix (the text of which we will examine momentarily), Aquinas again uses the language of final causality, this time concerning the nature of the act of faith considered as meritorious. As seen in the text (below), the language of being *moved by God through grace* [*moto a Deo per gratiam*], while being *subject to a free choice* [*subiictur libero arbitrio*], and standing wit*h a relation-toward God* [*relatus in Deum*]⁹⁰ all emphasizes *final causality* on God's part, and co-proximate *efficient causality* on the part of the willing subject. This language allows Aquinas to meet the criteria set forth for the character of merit in II-II.23.ii, which we examined above. These are:

1) that the act is voluntary, i.e. the mind [*mens*] is an active source of motion; and
2) that the will has power of itself to act or not.

I-II.114.i. adds these criteria:

3) that the act is something which *ought* to be done (from *ad* 1), and
4) that there is toil or work.

I-II.114.iii–iv reinforce points 1 and 2, while I-II.21.iii–iv, holding that merit or demerit is consequent upon the goodness or evil of an act, reinforce point 3. With the causal framework of theological virtue presented here considered in light of these criteria for meritorious action, we can now speak meaningfully about the merit of theological virtue, since without denying the metaphysical *priority* of God's efficient causality in the human will, we see the will itself to be the *co-proximate* efficient cause of its own intrinsically good activity. When I-II.114.i is brought together with I-II.10.iv and II-II.23.ii, we have the passage to which we made reference above: II-II.2.ix. In his *responsio*,

---

90. Our attention is directed again to two passages which have been previously discussed in the present volume: first, *Summa Theologiae* I.45.iii, where Aquinas discusses the being-constituting relation of the creature to God, and *Summa Theologiae* II-II.2.ii, where Aquinas distinguishes between the three senses of the term *credere*, and classifies the life of faith as *credere in Deum*, i.e. *to believe unto God*. In this phrase, like the phrase *relatus in Deum*, directionality and forward movement eliciting from *within* the human will are suggested. See again n. 80 in this study.

Aquinas speaks of the meritorious character of the act of faith:

> As stated above (I-II.114.iii–iv), our acts are meritorious in so far as they proceed from a free-will that is moved by God through grace. Every human act, then, that is subject to a free-choice, if it is with a *relation-toward* God, can be meritorious. Now, *to believe* is an act of the intellect assenting to the divine truth by virtue of the command of the will as moved by God through grace; and in this way it is subject to a free-will directed toward God. Therefore the act of faith can be meritorious.[91]

The argument is quite clear, and returns us to the central paradox under discussion. For the Predestinarian, the claim of merit is presumed from the outset to be absurd, since God is so far beyond us in power and in dignity that we cannot establish a degree of equality that would allow for merit. One cannot *merit* unless what one *does*, or what one *is*, is proportionate to the reward received, or to the one giving the reward. We cannot say that any such proportionality exists between the creature and God. Thus in denying free-will on the basis of God's omnipotence the Predestinarian finds no difficulty. As he sees it, free-will is not needed to secure merit since, by virtue of the disproportion between creature and Creator, merit is impossible anyway. For such a thinker, there is thus no sense in arguing for a free-will with all its metaphysical mire, since it serves no moral function without merit, and in the absence of the idea of *co-proximate* causality, cannot be seen to contribute anything relevant to the process of salvation. The consistency of these arguments is, for a Thomist, rather gruesome. Though formally *valid*, they rely upon premises Aquinas would not accept. True, no human being can approach God's perfection, ontologically speaking, but does that mean that we are wholly incapable of any degree of similarity? The tradition says no, that with the help of grace "we shall be made like him" (1 John 3:2), that in the blessed is found God's very

---

91. Dicendum quod, sicut supra dictum est, actus nostri sunt meritorii inquantum procedunt ex libero arbitrio moto a Deo per gratiam. Unde omnis actus humanus qui subiicitur libero arbitrio, si sit relatus in Deum, potest meritorius esse. Ipsum autem credere est actus intellectus assentientis veritati divinae ex imperio voluntatis a Deo motae per gratiam, et sic subiacet libero arbitrio in ordine ad Deum. Unde actus fidei potest esse meritorius.

likeness, which makes us "adopted sons" (Rom. 8:23), and "co-heirs" of the promise of Christ (Rom. 8:17). Thus we can merit before God through grace, which brings the "indwelling" of the Holy Spirit to the human person in the theological virtue of charity.

This, indeed, will be Aquinas' claim, held without prejudice to *Summa Theologiae* II-II.2.ix. In the first objection of that article, Aquinas gives this *counter*-argument to the argument put forth in the passage cited above:

> It seems that to believe is not meritorious. Indeed, the principle of merit is charity, as stated above (ibid. I-II.114.iv). But faith is a prelude to charity, as is nature. Thus, just as a natural act is not meritorious, since we do not merit by virtue of the natural, neither is an act of faith.[92]

Aquinas replies:

> *Nature* is compared to charity, which is the principle of merit, as *matter* to *form*; *faith* is compared to charity as a *prior disposition* to the ultimate form. It is clear that a subject or matter [which can only exercise agency through the power of form, of course,] cannot exercise agency through the power of form *before the form has come*; and neither can a disposition. But once the form *has* come, a subject and a prior disposition do exercise agency through the power of form, the *first principle* of agency. For example, the heat of fire exercises agency through the power of the substantial form [of fire]. In this way, therefore, neither *nature*, nor [even] *faith without charity*, is able to produce a meritorious act; but charity *soaring-above*, the act of faith, [precisely] on account of [this] charity, is made meritorious, just as is an act of nature and of natural free-will.[93]

---

92. Videtur quod credere non sit meritorium. Principium enim merendi est caritas, ut supra dictum est. Sed fides est praeambula ad caritatem, sicut et natura. Ergo, sicut actus naturae non est meritorius (quia naturalibus non meremur), ita etiam nec actus fidei.

93. [N]atura comparatur ad caritatem, quae est merendi principium, sicut materia ad formam. Fides autem comparatur ad caritatem sicut dispositio praecedens ultimam formam. Manifestum est autem quod subiectum vel

In what sense, however do we "merit" what we merit before God? To answer this question, we must turn first to *Summa Theologiae* I-II.114. In the first article of this question, Aquinas draws an indispensable distinction between "simple" and "relative" merit. The former exists when two equals stand before one another, and one performs some work for the other. In that case, where there is a *simple* equality, there is also a *simple* merit. In the case of a parent-child relationship, in which the child has no intrinsic authority to decide what will be served for dinner, the child may merit some degree of decision-making on that score *relatively* by virtue of doing something which the parent has promised to reward. In this case, there is a *relative* justice, and a *relative* merit. It is in this way that a human being can merit the rewards of salvation. In this case, it is not so much that God is being just to *us*, but to himself, "inasmuch as what is owed is that what he sets in order should be brought to fulfillment" (ibid. *ad* 3).[94] But the analogy is imperfect, since in the case of the relationship of the human being to God, the human being has no ontological autonomy—that is, as human beings we are dependent upon God for our very act of existence. Even a *relative* merit is, admittedly, rather difficult to fathom under these circumstances. In clarification of this point, Aquinas writes in his *responsio*:

> Now the mode and measure of human virtue is in the human being from God. Therefore, a human being's merit before God is not possible except on the presupposition of the divine ordination, so that, ironically, through his operation, a human being receives as a *sort of* wage from God, that *for* which God

---

materia non potest agere in virtute formae, neque etiam dispositio praecedens, antequam forma adveniat. Sed postquam forma advenerit, tam subiectum quam dispositio praecedens agit in virtute formae, quae est principale agendi principium: sicut calor ignis agit in virtute formae substantialis. Sic ergo neque natura neque fides sine caritate possunt producere actum meritorium: sed caritate superveniente, actus fidei fit meritorius per caritatem, sicut et actus naturae et naturalis liberi arbitrii.

94. The full text of *ad* 3 reads, "Ad tertium dicendum quod, quia actio nostra non habet rationem meriti nisi ex praesuppositione divinae ordinationis, non sequitur quod Deus efficiatur simpliciter debitor nobis, sed sibi ipsi: inquantum debitum est ut sua ordinatio impleatur."

gave him the power of operation. In the same way, natural things receive, by their proper movements and operations, that to which they were ordained by God—differently, indeed, because the rational creature moves *itself* to agency by its free-choice, whence its action has the ratio of *merit*, which is not so in other creatures. (Ibid. I-II.114.i)[95]

From this passage, it is clear that we cannot merit without God, since the argument rests upon the acknowledgment that God rewards us for doing what God himself enables us to do. Remove from the equation so-called "enabling grace" and the question of merit is altogether closed. Thus, I-II.114.ii asks *whether without grace it is possible for anyone to merit eternal life*, to which Aquinas responds in the negative. In Article iii, he asks about a central point: *whether by grace it is possible for anyone to merit eternal life out of condignity*. The Latin, *ex condigno*, means, roughly, *out of shared dignity*. In the *sed contra* of the article, Aquinas says that a condign reward is one "returned in accordance with a just judgement" [*redditur secundum iustum iudicium*]. Pointing to 2 Tim. 4:8, he says that life everlasting, which is called a "crown of justice" [*corona iustitiae*] granted by a "just judge" [*iustus iudex*], is thus, a *condign reward*. But justice, as we have said, presupposes some sort of equality—an equality which is only possible by the power of grace.

As a *quasi-formal cause* of the human will, charity is, in fact, *for us*, a *quality* inhering in the will as in a subject. Since, however, that quality is, in itself, the Holy Spirit, charity is a quality *ontologically nobler* than the subject in which it inheres. Aquinas writes in II-II.23.iii *ad* 3:

> Every quality, according to its being, is inferior to substance because substance is a being in itself, but quality [a being] in

---

95. Modus autem et mensura humanae virtutis homini est a Deo. Et ideo meritum hominis apud Deum esse non potest nisi secundum praesuppositionem divinae ordinationis: ita scilicet ut id homo consequatur a Deo per suam operationem quasi mercedem, ad quod Deus ei virtutem operandi deputavit. Sicut etiam res naturales hoc consequuntur per proprios motus et operationes, ad quod a Deo sunt ordinatae. Differenter tamen: quia creatura rationalis seipsam movet ad agendum per liberum arbitrium, unde sua actio habet rationem meriti; quod non est in aliis creaturis.

another. But according to the order of species, a quality caused by and originated in a subject, is less noble than its subject as effect is [less noble] than cause. However, when a quality is caused in a subject by its participating in something of a higher nature, that quality is nobler than the subject [in which it inheres], because it is a likeness of the superior nature, as light to a transparent body. In this way, charity is nobler than the soul, inasmuch as it is a certain participation [of the soul] in the Holy Spirit.[96]

This, therefore, is the root of merit. The soul is made capable through this *supra-natural* quality of meriting the rewards of salvation out of *condignity*. God's presence in the soul allows the soul to participate in God's own goodness and love, and gives the soul a likeness to him who dwells there. Yet, as a theological virtue, charity remains *our* activity, inasmuch as it empowers *our* free-will for the exercise of *our* supra-natural free choice for God. Though this choice is *our* choice, it is a choice made possible in us only by God's act of indwelling grace, raising us to a *new fullness*, while giving us an "inner excitement" by his inviting us to himself.

For this reason, Aquinas maintains that acts (even morally good acts) considered simply as proceeding from the free-will, *without reference to charity*, do not merit the rewards of salvation out of condignity. On the contrary, free-will acts only merit *condign* reward when the free-will from which they proceed is informed by charity. This is because, as we have said, any condignity between God and the human-being is derived from the Holy Spirit dwelling within us in the theological virtue of charity, and by grace, drawing our acts to their ontological fulfillment. Aquinas states:

> The worth of the work follows upon the dignity of grace,

---

96. [O]mne accidens secundum suum esse est inferius substantia: quia substantia est ens per se, accidens autem in alio. Sed secundum rationem suae speciei, accidens quidem quod causatur ex principiis subiecti est indignius subiecto, sicut effectus causa. Accidens autem quod causatur ex participatione alicuius superioris naturae est dignius subiecto, inquantum est similitudo superioris naturae: sicut lux diaphano. Et hoc modo caritas est dignior anima, inquantum est participatio quaedam Spiritus Sancti.

whereby a human being, in being made to share in the divine nature, is adopted as a son of God, to whom the inheritance is due by right of adoption, according to Rom. 8:17: *If sons, heirs also*. (ibid. I-II.114.iii)[97]

If, however, the Holy Spirit is only our *quasi-formal cause*—i.e. our formal cause only in an *analogous* sense—our *condignity* before God must also be understood *analogously*. In the strictest sense of the phrase, we do not *under any circumstances* "merit" before God out of *human* condignity with the divine essence. Rather, human beings, by a human act of will, "merit" out of *divine* condignity with the divine essence, through the indwelling of the Holy Spirit—*the relationship for which we were made*. When, in other words, we live within the context of a *relationship of intimacy* with the Holy Spirit, we are fulfilled in what we are, and "merit" before God through the *divine term* of that relationship, out of *condignity* with the divine essence. This "merit," however, remains *relative* because we, as human beings, bring before God only what God himself *enables* us to bring (ibid. i, iii).

In this context, then, the term *merit* is not to be understood as a *natural right* to which God is held morally bound in his dealings with us. To suggest this would be to render the divine essence subordinate to a power external to itself, which is absurd. Rather, merit *ought* to be understood as a *divine right* operative within the context of a relationship *involving* the creature, and *allowing* for the creature's *agency*. It is in this sense that our actions can be seen, in a meaningful way, as *meritorious* before God. It is through God's own nature—with which the human will is *bound-up* through the indwelling—that *our* actions *share the dignity* of the divine essence.

For Aquinas, this fact carries with it certain implications for just *what* we can merit out of that condignity. He discusses this issue at Summa Theologiae I-II.114.iii,v–x. There, Aquinas argues that through the grace of the indwelling, a human being can "merit" the following rewards: 1) an increase in grace for himself, 2) the goods necessary to attain to eternal life, 3) whatever material goods are necessary for the

---

97. Attenditur etiam pretium operis secundum dignitatem gratiae, per quam homo, consors factus divinae naturae, adoptatur in filium Dei, cui debetur hereditas ex ipso iure adoptionis, secundum illud *Rom.* 8: [17]: *Si filii, et heredes*.

performance of any work to which God has called this person, and 4) the reward of eternal life. All of these goods can be merited out of *condignity*, because the *good* which the *Holy Spirit* deserves by *divine right*, is *eternal felicity in the fellowship of God*. All of these goods are ordained to *that* end, such that the *Holy Spirit* deserves them, and so, *we who are bound-up with the Holy Spirit* deserve them on his account. This is an important point. We are *bound-up with* the Holy Spirit such that what the *Holy Spirit* deserves, *we* deserve because of him.

Of importance, here, is the fact that human beings *cannot* merit the *first grace*, the grace of *repentance*, or the grace of *perseverance of the course* [*perseverantia viae*]. Aquinas' views on these issues are to the point of any ecumenical discussion of the relationship between *human agency* and *divine causality* with respect to salvation. No real claim can be made, from a Thomistic line of reasoning, to what has typically been called "works-righteousness" or the idea that a human being *earns justification (from sin) through the performance of good works*. Aquinas' position is clear in the insistence that *grace* is a *prerequisite* and *co-requisite* for *condign merit* before God. We can, in other words, only merit on the basis of what is *already done in us* by the indwelling of the Holy Spirit. While the *first grace* must be *followed upon* by our agency if it is to be finally efficacious for us is a claim that must be made distinct from any implication that the *first grace itself* can be merited by us in any way. Even our *seeking after* truth must be seen, not as a *first cause* of our own, but as a *response to a first and persisting grace* given by God, which provides, as has been said, an *inner excitement soliciting unto belief*. Likewise, should a human being fall from grace through a deliberate choice, that human being may *turn again* to God, but *only because God reaches out* to the human being, *rousing* that person to repentance.

THE QUESTION OF PERSEVERANCE: SUGGESTIONS FOR A DIFFERENT APPROACH

We turn, now, to the question of perseverance. As we will see, an examination of Aquinas' thought on this subject (in particular, so-called *perseverance of the course*), reveals a current in his thinking that remains, in spite of all that we have seen up to this point, quite firmly

Predestinarian. We will endeavor, therefore, to suggest a different approach. That being said, the Catholic mind is rather consistent in holding that, while human beings *can* merit an increase in grace, *and whatever is necessary for salvation, we cannot merit perseverance of the course*, in particular, at the final hour. To say this, for Catholics, is to venture into the realm of mystery. *Mystery*, however, does not mean outright *contradiction*; and theologians have the task, therefore, of finding ways to consider the issue that do not end in ruin, but instead, capture the heart of the truth at stake in the doctrine. Aquinas, for his part, approaches the mystery of perseverance as follows:

> Since a human being naturally has a free-will, bendable toward good and evil, there are two possible ways to obtain perseverance in good from God. One way indeed [is] by that which *determines* the free-will to good—that is, by *consummate grace*, which will occur in glory. Another way [is by that which] comes entirely from the *divine motion* which *inclines* the human being to good *right up to the very end*. As is clear from what was said [earlier], however (vi–viii), that comes under human merit which is bound-up with the motion of the free-will directed by God, who moves it as its *terminus*. [This is] *not* [the case], however, with what is bound-up with the aforesaid motion as *principle*. Whence it is clear that the perseverance of glory, which is the *terminus* of the aforementioned motion, comes under merit. Perseverance *of the course*, however, does *not* come under merit, [because] this [perseverance] depends solely upon the *divine* motion, which is the *principle* of all merit. Nonetheless, God *lavishes* the good of perseverance upon whichever one he lavishes it, *with no recompense at all*. (I-II.114.ix)[98]

---

98. [C]um homo naturaliter habeat liberum arbitrium flexibile ad bonum et ad malum, dupliciter potest aliquis perseverantiam in bono obtinere a Deo. Uno quidem modo, per hoc quod liberum arbitrium determinatur ad bonum per gratiam consummatam: quod erit in gloria. Alio modo, ex parte motionis divinae, quae hominem inclinat ad bonum usque in finem. Sicut autem ex dictis patet, illud cadit sub humano merito, quod comparatur ad motum liberi arbitrii directi a Deo movente, sicut terminus: non autem id quod comparatur ad praedictum motum sicut principium. Unde patet quod perseverantia gloriae, quae est terminus, praedicti motus, cadit sub merito: perseverantia autem viae

The English Dominicans employ the term *final perseverance* in their translation[99] of this article; but it should be noted that Aquinas himself does not rely upon such a category, explicitly, in his own text. The term *final perseverance* is intended to draw-out the distinction Aquinas makes between the *perseverance of glory* which *determines* the will to the good for eternity, and *simple* perseverance *in this life* which merely *inclines* the will to the good, but does *not* determine it. Likewise, when Aquinas uses the phrase *usque in finem* (right to the very end), his emphasis is placed upon the fact that human beings tend to sin, periodically, throughout life, and then to repent again by God's grace. Catholic usage of this terminology has, as its central concern, not the hopelessness of a predestinarian "sweepstakes of salvation and damnation", but instead, an urgent caution against the sin of *presumption*, whereby we divest ourselves of any *personal* responsibility to make right use of the power of grace, and to cling to God in love at every moment. For Aquinas, what is at issue, at this precise moment in his discussion, is not whether God will *abandon* a human being at the final hour, but whether, *over the course of life*, God always inclines the human will to the good so vigorously as to *determine* it to that end. Aquinas holds that God does *not* do this. Rather, he allows human beings to turn their intellectual gaze *away from* the light of his grace which, so long as they would choose to *behold* it, would *incline them to the good*. Where God allows the light of grace to illumine the human intellect, however, and to thus incline the will, God is acting, not *in response* to us, but on his own *initiative* as a free and autonomous person who comes and goes as he pleases.[100]

---

non cadit sub merito, quia dependet solum ex motione divina, quae est principium omnis meriti. Sed Deus gratis perseverantiae bonum largitur, cuicumque illud largitur.

99. St. Thomas Aquinas, *Summa Theologica* (3 vols.), Fathers of the English Dominican Province, trans., (New York: Benzinger Brothers, Inc., 1947).

100. As far as this articulation takes us, *perseverance of the course* (in particular, as it is received in the final moments of life) might manifest itself, in particular cases, in the mystical encounter known as "resting in the spirit"—the phenomenon typically, though not exclusively, associated with an engagement of one gifted with the special charism of *healing*. It should be noted that this

As Aquinas makes clear throughout the other articles in Question 114, however, while in a state of grace, we *merit*, and are *given* by God, whatever help we need to attain eternal life. Now, as we have said, Aquinas elsewhere suggests a rather Predestinarian view on this point—one that favors eternal security on the grounds of God's immutability and omnipotence. We are left, here, however, to consider the claim that God provides, on account of the merit of grace, all that is necessary to attain eternal life. Herein lies a difficulty. We *need perseverance* in grace if we are, finally, to be *saved* by grace and gain eternal life. In what sense, then, can perseverance be considered a *gift* for one *already* justified? If, as Aquinas holds, the just person merits an *increase* in grace, *preservation* in that grace would seem all the more an object of merit. As Aquinas sees it, however, perseverance "right to the very end" is not at all an object of merit, because it is a *precondition* for merit, since it is, precisely, perseverance in the grace *whereby* we merit everything else. But if, in a state of grace, we merit all that we require to attain eternal life in the end, would it not seem that, *principle* of movement or *terminus* of movement, if perseverance of the course is itself *necessary* for the attainment of eternal life, we do, indeed, *merit* it, and God *always* provides it, in justice, to those who do not spurn the indwelling of the Holy Spirit through concrete mortal sin?

Let us consider the issue from a different perspective. If, in grace, we

---

ecstatic translation of the human consciousness to divine intimacy comes in the best tradition of Catholic mysticism, and should not be understood as a mere *psychological affect* reserved for the emotionally-charged arena of charismatic style praise services. Many great Catholic saints appear to have experienced this translation on (sometimes frequent) occasion. Among many others, we may name: Maximus the Confessor, Francis, Dominic, Bonaventure, Catherine of Sienna, Theresa of Avila, Padre Pio, and, we suggest, Thomas Aquinas. In this experience, human awareness of God as a distant, background reality giving context and meaning to the material, sensible world of which we are normally vividly aware, *advances suddenly to the foreground of our consciousness*, while what is normally in the foreground recedes into the background. In this state, one is not, necessarily, wholly unaware of the material, sensible world—indeed, one may be acutely attuned to it in comparison to ordinary consciousness; more to the point, the sensible world simply pales in comparison to the mystical encounter, which, for as long as it lasts, is invariably preferred to all else. Those who minister to the dying might consider whether such an account might explain some of their observations.

merit all that is required for the attainment of eternal life, and perseverance *cannot* be merited under any circumstance, even in the state of grace, it would seem to be, not so much a *necessary* help in the attainment of eternal life, but an extraordinary divine favor which makes it not only *possible* for us to choose God, but *highly likely* that we will.[101] Aquinas does not seem to hold this view; but even if he did, we would be left, on such a model, with the rather odd suggestion that one might attain eternal life without actually *persevering*. This view could be justified by insisting upon a distinction between the *grace* of perseverance, regarded as a special divine favor, and the concrete *fact* of perseverance, which might be realized even in the *absence* of a special favor. Still, the Tradition does not speak of perseverance in quite this sense, and a theologian would speculate too boldly to propose such a thesis, publicly, at this point in the dialogue.

For Aquinas, of course, *perseverance* means, simply, *not sinning*. This position is problematic, however, for it seems to require that God, by *withholding* perseverance from those in a state of grace, not only *abandons* the faithful, but actually *coerces* the faithful to mortal sin. We realize, of course, that such a suggestion is clearly contrary to Catholic teaching, and to Aquinas' own intentions, but the supporting argument does possess, nonetheless, a certain veracity. If *to persevere* is simply *not to sin*, then to *not* persevere is nothing other than to *sin*, actually and personally. Thus, if we *cannot* persevere without some

---

101. Neither in the contemporary *Catechism of the Catholic Church* (§2016) nor in the Council of Trent's *Decree Concerning Justification* (XIII and Canon 16), do we see the depiction of so-called "final perseverance" as something that God might *withdraw* from the human person. Instead, the question is whether God will allow us to withdraw *ourselves* from *his grace* in the last hour. The doctrine we have come to know as "final perseverance" is actually directed against the claim of "eternal security," as the Decree's Canon 16 reveals. According to Aquinas and the larger Church, God *could* "fix" us to his grace such that, in the absence of any competing motive of action, we are *unable* to turn away from him; but there is no guarantee that he will do so. Aquinas suggests, however, that because the grace of the indwelling *empowers* us to freely choose him of our own agency, God's decision *not* to "fix" my will in the last hour does not constitute an abandonment, since it does not deny me what I need to choose him—it only *allows me to retain* what I need to *reject* him—namely, competing motives of action, which, of themselves, cannot compel me to sin.

special gift of God's unmerited grace, then, on Aquinas' model, we are required to affirm that unless God intervenes to *impede* personal sin, personal sin *cannot be avoided*. It is, therefore, on this model, difficult to see how personal sin, might really fall, authentically, under the category of a *human act*, properly so-called, since the very *ratio* of a human act is to be voluntary and deliberate, and thus *avoidable*—and, for that reason alone, deserving of praise or blame, reward or reprobation. Furthermore, to say that *personal sin* cannot be avoided, is necessarily to say that we are *determined* to sin *concretely*. In that case, we must affirm the doctrine of *double-predestination* and confess that some are made for heaven and others for hell by God's eternal plan of creation. This, however, is precisely the position we seek to avoid.

Fortunately, however, Catholic teaching on the question of perseverance has always allowed room for a variety of opinions, and has stopped short of affirming a strictly Thomistic view of the matter. It might be better, for instance, to consider the issue in relation to God's power to govern the bounds of human life—to preserve a particular life until a movement toward repentance might realize fulfillment, or to bring an end to one's journey while the will is firmly fixed to God in love. Such a model leaves open the mystery of the human heart, and the possibility that, according to a plan knowable only to God, each human life might either, through God's favor, come to an end at an opportune time, or else be guarded by God, who does not abandon his creature, until that creature, of its own authority and by its own choice, fixes the will definitively and irrevocably in refusal of God's overflowing mercy.

That being said, perseverance is, indeed, a *paradox*. It would seem to be both necessary for salvation *and* unmerited, while, at the same time, remaining a category applicable only to those already *actually* justified, and thus, *due*, by grace, whatever is required for the attainment of eternal life. To understand the issue correctly, we should, again, be certain to remember that we are dealing, here, with the dynamics of an interpersonal relationship—the relationship within which the creature abides with God in grace. As a relationship, the life of grace must be *cultivated*; it tends to grow stronger with that cultivation, provided both parties are well engaged, or else to atrophy if cultivation of the relationship is neglected. God, for his own part, cultivates this relationship through the promptings of the spirit, sacramental intervention, and other so-called "actual graces." The human being cultivates this relationship through *cooperation* with those graces, and this, by virtue of that infusion of undergirding power for supernatural operation they comport. In prayer, we turn to God *relationally*, petitioning him for a free outpouring of love, asking, first above all, to be received by him in love, *now, and in the moment of our final breath*. We appeal, in other words, to the radical freedom of divine generosity. We cannot *merit* this reception; but because God *reveals* himself to us as an overflowing font of inexhaustible mercy, the paternal and spousal exemplar of steadfast love and fidelity, we can be sure in our hope that he *will*, in fact, grant us what we ask, if what we ask is to *abide in his love* according to his explicit command (cf. John 15:1–11).

Let us consider the issue in another way. Human beings, we might say, can never strictly *merit* from God, even on the basis of the indwelling, that he *show* himself to us, or *be* for us, in any *particular* way, just as by *human* friendships we do not *merit* our friend's acceptance of an invitation, extension of an invitation, or unbidden assistance. Rather, as a free and autonomous person, our friend may come and go as he pleases, though we certainly *enjoy the right to call upon him* as a privilege of friendship, and can morally expect from our friend a certain *responsiveness to our needs*. That expectation, however, in certain instances, rests not upon the basis of any rights-claim on our part, but upon the basis of our friend's *fidelity*, our friend's *generosity*, and our friend's *largesse*—it is much more about our *friend*, in those instances, than it is about us. Indeed, what our friend will do for us *wholly out of an outpouring of love*, manifest in the realization of an unmerited spontaneous initiative, is a question quite distinct from that of strict justice—yet rather than diminishing our appreciation of the richness of our relationship, this dynamic constitutes much of the *enjoyment* of friendship, over and above friendship's strictly *moral* character.

Again, we emphasize, here, the radically personal character of God—the fact that, since God is a free and autonomous person, we cannot *demand* that he come to us, nor can we strictly *merit* his personal self-outpouring in any way. This, indeed, is precisely the point of the commandment against taking the name of God in vain. If the name *Yahweh* means, not so much *static being*, but *uncoerced being*, or *One who cannot be controlled*, then we are reminded that any attempt to *conjure* God, and make him *do for us* or *be for us* according to our own personal desire or necessity, is really a form of idolatry; for no *conjured* god can ever be the God of the burning bush: the God of Abraham, of Isaac, and of Jacob (cf. Exod 3:1–4:17). By entering into covenant with us, God gives us the right to call upon him, even as sons to a Father, but he does not, thereby, cease to be *Yahweh*, the Great Eternal Thou. He may, in the end, do as we ask, but wholly of his own accord.

In his *Introduction to Christianity*, Joseph Ratzinger, who has since been elevated to the Chair of Peter as Pope Benedict XVI, frames the issue in precisely this sort of interpersonal, relational language. He suggests that the root fact of a Christian anthropology in which the human person is meant for interpersonal relationship—and ultimately for a relationship with God—places us in an unavoidable position of radical vulnerability. Because we are *for the other*, he argues, we can never really find our fulfillment, even if *we*, for our own part, are ready to pour ourselves out to the other completely, unless, that is, the other is prepared to *receive* us in that outpouring. But the fact that the one *to whom* we pour ourselves out is also a *person*—a free and autonomous agent—means, in the end, that the *reception* of our self-gift depends *entirely* upon the other's radically self-governed willingness to receive it freely and without coercion. Whether or not we are fulfilled depends, that is to say, upon the will of the other *for whom* we lay bear our soul's deepest vulnerabilities. He writes:

> Being a Christian means essentially changing over from being for oneself to being for one another. This also explains what is really meant by the rather odd-seeming concept of election ("predestination"). It does not mean a preference that leaves the individual undisturbed in himself and divides him from the others, but entrance on the common task of which we spoke earlier [namely, creative, sacrificial self-offering through the power of the Crucified Christ]. Accordingly, the basic Christian decision signifies the assent to being a Christian, the abandonment of self-centeredness and accession to Jesus Christ's existence with its concentration on the whole....
>
> In conclusion it must be stated that all man's own efforts to step outside himself can never suffice. He who only wants to give and is not ready to receive, he who only wants to exist for others and is unwilling to recognize that he for his part too lives on the unexpected, unprovokable gift of others' "For", fails to recognize the basic mode of human existence and is thus bound

to destroy the true meaning of living "for one another". To be fruitful, all self-sacrifices demand acceptance by others and in the last analysis by *the* other who is the truly "other" of all mankind and at the same time completely one with it: the God-man Jesus Christ.[102]

To frame this mystery-cluster of *predestination, election,* and *final perseverance* in these terms is, we suggest, to liberate the gospel message—the message of the Incarnation of a God who genuinely seeks the salvation of his creature, even to the point of dying for his creature on the Cross. Such a God commands a public proclamation of the Good News of the offer of salvation, not simply to those who will finally answer it and persevere in fact, but to *everyone*, with the implication that this announcement of grace itself includes the grace announced, such that *anyone* and *everyone* can respond to it. Such a proclamation would seem to demand the exclusion of any under-the-breath qualification to the effect that what is announced may not, in fact, apply to *this* particular individual in God's preconceived plan for the universe. For as Pope John Paul II insists in his encyclical *Dives in Misericordia*, the heart of the Gospel itself is really the very Incarnation of the *hanan* or *chânan*[103] of God. He reminds us, on this score, that:

> we have inherited from the Old Testament—as it were in a special synthesis—not only the wealth of expressions used by those books in order to define God's mercy, but also a specific and obviously anthropomorphic "psychology" of God: the image of His anxious love, which in contact with evil, and in particular with the sin of the individual and of the people, is manifested as mercy. This image is made up not only of the rather general content of the verb *hanan* [or *chânan*] but also of the content of *hesed* [or *chesed*] and *rahamim* [or *rachamim*]. The term *hanan* [*chânan*] expresses a wider concept: it

---

102. Joseph Cardinal Ratzinger, *Introduction to Christianity*, J. R. Foster, trans., (San Francisco: Communio Books/Ignatius Press, 1969, 1990), 190–191.

103. *The Mercy of God: Dives in Misericordia*, 30 November, 1980, Vatican translation, (Boston: St. Paul Books & Media, 1980), § 4, n. 52. My *emphasis*.

means in fact the manifestation of grace, which involves, so to speak, a constant predisposition to be generous, benevolent and merciful.[104]

The term *chesed* indicates *an overflowing goodness*—one that reaches beyond the parameters of a legal agreement or the requirements of strict justice, and reveals the *faithfulness* of the Person who stands betrayed, yet, in the face of that betrayal, remains willing to live out and even to restore the relationship the other has wounded or destroyed by sin. The term *rachamim* is still more anthropomorphic. It indicates *a motherly love*—one, by nature, heart-felt and affective, and which longs, above all else, to reconcile with the wayward child who had once nestled in his mother's womb, suckled at her breast, and took comfort at her gentle touch. Typically, however, Christian philosophers are inclined, in their commitment to reconciling faith with reason, to qualify these concepts until they are thoroughly emptied of their anthropomorphic content. But, as a word of caution, in *Dives in Misericordia*, at least, John Paul II does not suggest this approach. Instead, he appeals to those very anthropomorphisms for evidence of the true content of God's self-revelation in Jesus Christ. He is, of course, aware of the profound philosophical difficulties this represents, and thus speaks, throughout, of the "*mystery* of mercy" which it is the Church's express duty to safeguard and proclaim, without hesitation and without qualification, especially in the present age. Thus, while we must be certain to integrate faith and reason if we hope to present a theology that can call itself authentically Catholic, we must also be certain to maintain the priority of revelation over what reason can naturally comprehend, ever mindful of the fact that revelation, "pushes philosophy to its limits, as reason is summoned to make its own a logic which brings down the walls within which it risks being confined."[105] We must, of course, acknowledge that God reveals divine truth in human language and human modes of thought. Nevertheless, what revelation says about God must still be seen as something more than a collection of statements about human beings and how we respond to him. Even in these anthro-

---

104. Ibid.

105. John Paul II, *Fides et Ratio: On the Relationship between Faith and Reason*, September 14, 1998, Vatican translation, (Boston: Pauline Books & Media, 1998), § 80.

pomorphic representations, the Scriptures are *God's self-revelation*—they do communicate something true about *God*. Indeed, it is precisely for this reason that some, today, are prepared to re-examine the concept of *receptivity* as a positive perfection rather than a pure passivity as it is in the thinking of Aquinas.[106] While it is clearly beyond the scope of the present study to enter upon that debate, we must emphasize that inquiries of this type are, for the reasons we have mentioned, as important as they are daunting.

That being said, if we follow the example of John Paul II, a proper integration of faith and reason would seem to require an approach that allows revelation to retain the full measure of its richness and profundity in light of new insights into the perennial questions of human existence. In the present study, we have sought to be faithful to this endeavor, presenting, we contend, a coherent, if still somewhat incomplete, theology of human cooperation and dependency that avoids both Pelagianism and Predestinarianism on solid philosophical grounds, true to the content of revelation. The approach we propose to this mystery, therefore, while not precisely that of Aquinas, is, still, quite firmly

---

106. We refer, here, to the idea of *active receptivity* suggested by Hans Urs von Balthasar. In his now famous lecture, *Person and Being*, W. Norris Clarke, S.J., himself a noted Thomist, expresses openness to the idea that Balthasar offers us a new and coherent approach to the categories of being. According to that approach, *receptivity* can be understood as a positive perfection compatible with the *actus purus* of the divine essence, rather than always and everywhere as a *negation* of perfection. The latter, of course, would be necessarily *incompatible* with any philosophically coherent conception of the divine. (See W. Norris Clarke, S.J., *Person and Being*, The Aquinas Lecture, 1993 [Milwaukee: Marquette University Press, 1993], 20–32, especially 20–24.) Clarke does not follow through on the broader metaphysical implications of this proposition, since his purpose is to explore the metaphysical underlayment of personhood. He rests on the observation that receptivity is a dimension of the Triune life of God, already, in a certain respect, recognized by Aquinas (though, we contend, more fully appreciated in Bonaventure). Still, if we choose to go further with this reasoning, we can see that the implications of Balthasar's proposal may have a tremendous degree of explanatory power, if articulated in a way that can withstand the obvious philosophical objection that seems, almost, to recommend *itself*—namely, that if, by *receptivity*, we mean some sort of affectivity on God's part, God is made, it would seem, to be dependent upon his creation, which is absurd.

rooted in the metaphysical apparatus he provides, but with a much more existentially compelling confidence in the proclamation of God's steadfast love and fidelity—his *chânan* and his *chesed*. This footing is, we suggest, better situated to help us deal honestly with the richness and mystery of God's profoundly personal Old Testament self-revelation, brought to its ultimate and unimaginable fulfillment in Jesus Christ. It allows us, we suggest, to preserve both human freedom and divine causality in the assent into the life of faith, such that we can, therefore, truly be said to merit the rewards of salvation, while remaining radically dependent upon God's merciful generosity, which alone makes possible the worthiness of our free acts of will.

Concluding Remarks

The Present Study and the Challenge of Ecumenical Diologue In a Post-Modern Society

In his work, *Mere Christianity*,[107] C. S. Lewis argues that if we employ a term too loosely, it eventually becomes meaningless. He argues that it is therefore important for the term *Christianity* to be used only as it has been classically defined—namely, as denoting adherence to the claim that human beings are given a Redeemer in Jesus of Nazareth, the God-Man, who alone has the power to reconcile us with the Father, through his historically genuine death and bodily resurrection. Unfortunately, Lewis' concerns have been well-founded. Today, people are frequently described as "Christian," not because of any precise doctrinal affirmation, nor because of any compelling *faith in,* or *reliance upon,* Christ, but because they embody *attitudes* of acceptance and kindness, which we have come to associate with Jesus. This so-called "ethical Christianity," which views Jesus principally as a moral example, may be called a kind of *Neopelagianism*.[108] Typically, "ethical Christianity" denies the need for any faith in Christ as the principle of our salvation. If it grants any supernatural reality at all, "ethical Christianity" counts on God's unconditional love to spare virtually

---

107. C. S. Lewis, *Mere Christianity*, revised and enlarged edition, (New York: Macmillan Publishing Co., 1952), 8–11.

108. *Neopelagianism* cannot be considered as a single perspective, but as a broad genus subsuming any number of perspectives, including some developments within "liberal Protestantism" (eudaimonism, rationalism, and natural religion) and popularizations of such thinkers as Schleiermacher, Kant, Hegel, Kierkegaard, Tillich and Rahner.

everyone from any judgment of eternal consequence. It is nearly a universalistic claim, therefore, taking final beatitude (if, that is, this concept is even retained) as a given, and reserving condemnation only for the most overtly savage human beings.[109] It is just as often an entirely secular perspective, which denies the literal sense of the claims of "divinity," "incarnation," and "resurrection" associated with the figure of Jesus.[110]

Across this spectrum, "ethical Christianity" frequently is reduced to any number of metaphysical positions from pantheism to atheism. Much of the so-called "New-Age" mentality falls under this genus of thought, which also defines the general sentiments of large segments of the population of the United States. Its great appeal is that it defuses inter-cultural tensions in our increasingly "integrated" society, by reducing all claims of metaphysical and moral truth to the status of Jamesian-Pragmatic affirmations of the individual "will to believe."[111]

---

109. For more on the topic of moral relativism as a characteristic presupposition in our contemporary Western society, see Richard H. Bulzacchelli, "Duns Scotus's Third Volitional Posture' and a Critique of the Problem of Moral Indifference in Our Time," *Franciscan Studies*, Vol. 58 (2000): 77–109. Part II of this article (96–106) concentrates upon the "critique."

110. For a brief treatment of this contemporary climate from a Roman Catholic perspective, see Richard John Neuhaus, *The Catholic Moment: the Paradox of the Church in the Modern World*, (San Francisco: Harper & Row, Publishers, 1987): 69–82. Also of relevance are, Allan Bloom, *The Closing of the American Mind*, (New York: Simon and Schuster, 1987), and Richard H. Bulzacchelli, "Duns Scotus Third Volitional Posture'," 96–106.

111. The author recalls a conversation in a social setting in which an interlocutor said that he did not care at all what one affirmed as a personal belief, so long as one believed in *something*. He, however, confessed to believing in nothing at all save the science of optics: the interlocutor's professional area of specialization. What we find most interesting here is the paternalism revealed in the commentator. The issue is not the *ad hominem* observation *that* the interlocutor patronizes the masses, but the legitimate criticism that he does so because he first rejects any epistemological framework sufficient to warrant intellectual assent to any truth the average person could understand. He thereby "poisons the well" of discourse, dismissing any framework for discussion other than the mathematico-scientistic arena. As a "scientist," the interlocutor has graduated beyond the naive perspective from which the average person views

Yet, the clearly un-Scriptural, and counter-traditional character of the various *Neopelagian* attitudes in contemporary society, which utterly relativize Christian faith and morality, has made Calvinist claims, for their distinct lack of ambiguity on the issue of divine Lordship, more widely appealing in recent years. This, in turn, has led to a boom in Calvinist-rooted evangelical Christianity.[112]

---

the world. From his "educated" point of view, he perceives an inability on the part of the *common* people to reach his *own* level of understanding, and desires for them instead, the best that *they* can achieve: belief in some *"mythos"* which the "scientist" knows to be a fairy-tale. This very attitude, which is fundamentally closed to dialogue, is the persistent nemesis throughout Chesterton's apologetical works.

112. So-called "mega-churches" are a growing phenomenon in the United States today. These enormous, and typically, non-denominational congregations, tend to assemble in theatre-like buildings where their pastors give extended lessons on the Scriptures of their choosing. By nature, these congregations are broadly Calvinistic, inasmuch as the worship structure they adopt is non-liturgical and non-sacramental in its approach. Christian radio stations, furthermore, are prevalent on all bandwidths, while the Sky Angel system presents a kind of common front of Christian and Christo-sympathetic television and audio broadcasts delivered via satellite. Most of these stations are dominated by Calvinist-rooted Christians such as Reformed, Baptist, and Presbyterian, as well as non-denominational ministers, frequently associated with "mega-churches". Indeed, in spite of the "televangelist" scandals of the late 1980's, use of telecommunications media for missionary activity from within the broadly Calvinist tradition seems more prevalent today than ever before. There is, it seems clear, an audience for the gospel message; and to the credit of their obedience, these evangelists are ready to reach out to them, if yet with a decidedly Calvinistic message. Overwhelmingly, the two doctrines most frequently and thoroughly expounded by these evangelists are *Biblical literal inerrancy* in the context of a *sola scriptura* assertion, and *salvation by faith alone and not by works of any kind*, which form the foundation of Calvinist Christianity. It should be noted well, however, that we make no claim, in this presentation, that all Calvinist-rooted evangelical Christians adhere to the consequent Calvinist doctrine of "double-predestination." Indeed, we hold that this view is *not* universally affirmed by these groups. Nonetheless, if Calvinism is *consistently* maintained, this doctrine is always near at hand.

We would be remiss, however, if, at this point, we neglected any mention of *Catholic* efforts to employ the power of the media. Indeed, it is altogether misleading to suggest that Calvinists, or Protestants more generally, are solely

There are obvious reasons for Calvinism's appeal in the face of what amounts to a permissive culture of *indifferentism* and *moral relativism*. The doctrines of Biblical literal inerrancy and double-predestination offer a clear alternative to the relativistic Neopelagianism of the larger society. They are, furthermore, whether authentic to apostolic Christianity or not, a *firm ground* upon which to build, restore, or at least *stabilize* a society, and so, offer a theoretical antidote to the social decay most Americans claim to perceive.

By contrast, the secularist, Neopelagian doctrines that we can "do for ourselves," "approach 'God' on our own terms," "make our own moral decisions," and "decide for ourselves what life is about," have not, in the end, it seems, led to a genuine satisfaction in the human search for meaning. Without, at this point, embarking upon a lengthy proof of a *causal* relationship between Neopelagianism and societal decline, we can easily note a *correlation in time* between the rise of this perspective and increases in all the major indicators of social discord and human misery. As Neopelagian attitudes have taken firmer hold in the American consciousness, we have seen increases in these indicators: teen pregnancy, un-wed pregnancy, abortion, divorce, sexually transmitted disease, violence, anxiety, depression, and suicide. In the face of this fact, many have begun a search for just the sort of certainty and so-called *vertical transcendence* the Predestinarian can offer.

In recent decades, Calvinism has, indeed, undergone a resurgence in the United States, in response to a declining sense of truth, meaning, and moral certainty as the cult of "personal freedom" continues to displace traditional cultural, social, and moral conventions. Also in recent years, however, some steps leading toward *union* rather than *division*

---

responsible for large-scale media activity. No one can ignore the media efforts of, for instance, Eternal Word Television Network (EWTN) and Family Land Network, brought forth in response to the Catholic Church's hopes that the mass-media, in particular, telecommunications media, might be employed for the work of evangelization. See the decree of the Second Vatican Council, *Inter Mirifica*, 4 December, 1963. See also, the Pastoral Instruction of the Pontifical Council for Instruments of Social Communication, *Communio et Progressio*, 29 January, 1971. These documents are available in English Translation in, Austin Flannery, O.P., ed., *The Conciliar and Post Conciliar Documents*, [Vatican Council II: vol. 1], (Northport, New York: Costello Publishing Company, Inc., 1996): 283–292 and 293–349 respectively.

have been taken by those invested in the question at issue in the present work. Many, even from Calvinist backgrounds, recognize today that beside Predestinarianism and Pelagianism, there are other lines of reasoning available to those who would participate in this discussion—other approaches to the search for certainty, which may come without the difficulties the Predestinarian must ultimately face.

Lutherans, for example, who have always rejected radical Predestinarianism, have always agreed with Catholics on two significant points: 1) that God causes faith, i.e. that faith comes through grace, and 2) that salvation is a gift of grace related to the gift of faith. Among the principal questions which remain to be settled between Catholics and Lutherans, however, is that of the *sense in which* God *causes* faith and *causes* salvation. Neither Catholics nor, as a group, Lutherans, hold to the extreme-Calvinist assertion of total human non-involvement.[113] Still, Catholics and Lutherans have traditionally disagreed with one another over the question of *merit* before God with respect to the rewards of salvation.[114] While Lutherans typically agree that human beings are in some sense *involved* in their own salvation, they have generally remained uncomfortable with the Catholic claim of "merit." This disagreement hinges upon the answer to the question of *causality*. If God causes salvation without the cooperation of the human person, there is no sense in which a human being can be said to *merit* anything before God. If, however, the human person *does* cooperate in the process of salvation, then we *can* say that in some sense we "merit" its rewards. Resistance to the claim of *merit*, then, tends to lead to a total denial of the claim of *human cooperation*. This fact is borne out both by Luther's own struggle to annunciate the role of the individual in the process of salvation, and in the historical fact of the tendency of early

---

113. Here we are not speaking of *Lutherans* as Luther and those who follow his literal teaching, but as those associated with the tradition grounded in the *Schwabach Articles*, the *Torgau Articles*, the *Augsburg Confession*, and the *Formula of Concord*. The *Formula of Concord*, for example, clearly holds open the possibility of human refusal of the gifts of grace (II.57–60). While denying any possibility for cooperation *prior* to "conversion", the Formula holds that cooperation can take place *after* "conversion."

114. We must always take great care to remember the distinction between meriting the *rewards of salvation* and meriting *justification*. The former is consistent with Catholic theology; but the latter is distinctly Pelagian.

Lutheran churches to drift into Calvinism.[115] This fact alone does not wholly invalidate Lutheran resistance to the claim of merit, however. One might suggest that the continuing uneasiness felt by most Lutherans on this point stems from an epidemic lack of clarity concerning the meaning of the term *merit* and its relationship to God's *causal* posture with respect to our salvation. Catholics and Lutherans must, each for their own part, accept responsibility for this lack of clarity.

It is fair to say, furthermore, that many contemporary Calvinist-based traditions no-longer insist upon a radical Predestinarianism. The (Presbyterian) Confession of 1967, for example, makes no mention of radical Predestinarianism. One hears in informal discussion, increasingly common references to a *universal offer of grace* which one might choose to accept or to reject. Even between Catholics and Calvinists today, it seems, dialogue is now open on this point, at least to the extent that many Calvinist-rooted Christians are increasingly prepared to accept that we may here be speaking of a *mystery* of which we cannot so very neatly dispose.

The years following the Second Vatican Council have been marked, especially, by great strides in the dialogue between *Catholics* and *Lutherans*. Especially in the past decade or two, with the success of recent inter-dialogue agreements, real *trust* has begun to develop between Catholics and Lutherans.[116] This has led to an openness on the part of many Lutherans to reclaim some previously rejected elements of the Church's tradition, including Scholastic theology.[117] It thus seems

---

115. The "Philippists" (followers of Philip of Hessia), tended toward Calvinism and gradually became thoroughly Calvinistic. Countries in which the Philippists were influential in popular piety also became Calvinistic. See George J. Fritschel, *The Formula of Concord: Its Origins and Contents* (Philadelphia, PA: The Lutheran Publication Society, 1916), 51–52, 57–58.

116. Of importance here is the series of publication-producing dialogues which includes, H. George Anderson, et al., eds., *Justification by Faith*, (Lutherans and Catholics in Dialogue: VII, Minneapolis: Augsburg Publishing House, 1985). More recently, we have seen the "Joint Declaration on the Doctrine of Justification," *Origins* (vol. 28:8, 1998): 120–127.

117. Shortly after the period of Melanchthon, Scholastic theology had fallen out of favor among Lutherans as a danger in solidifying errors. It came to be seen as too much the invention of the human mind, and without a sufficient grounding in Scripture, which was always to be preferred according to the *sola*

appropriate to look to that tradition for clarification on the questions of *merit* and *causality* with respect to the relationship between theological virtue and the rewards of salvation; and here, as we have proposed to the reader in the present study, Thomas Aquinas provides a very important key.

It is hoped that the present study may help to break down at least some of the ideological and conceptual barriers which have divided Christians for so long. Nonetheless, we recognize that such progress, while important, is but an initial step in the ecumenical dialogue. It is a beginning to the long and difficult project of surmounting the emotional and political obstacles which have taken centuries to erect. We do not, here, claim to have answered the question once and for all with a definitive resolution, but to have offered a meaningful framework within which to enter into further dialogue oriented toward ever-deepening insight into the mystery of redemption.

Perhaps, in the future, ecumenists across Christian denominational boundaries will be able to discuss the sovereignty of God's immediate causal activity without diminishing the significance of human moral agency. Perhaps, also, Christians might strive more earnestly to stress the significance of human responsibility without diminishing the supreme and immediate power of God in every moment of the creative-redemptive process. There exists promising evidence that this is already beginning to happen.

In the years preceding the publication of the present study, efforts of the post-Vatican II Catholic-Lutheran dialogue on the question at issue reached a new threshold in the appearance of their "Joint Declaration on the Doctrine of Justification." The significance of this contribution, as an ecumenical milestone, should not be underestimated. Still, an honest appraisal of the work requires the admission that the pivotal perspectival difference between the interlocutors remains a serious impediment to any claim of substantive agreement on the nature of God's causality in grace as it bears upon human free-will.[118] The idea

---

scriptura principle above any authority from Tradition, no matter how ancient or widely accepted. We cannot undertake a criticism of this position here.

118. For a discussion of this issue, see J. Malloy, "The Nature of Justifying Grace: A Lacuna in the *Joint Declaration*," *The Thomist*, vol. 65, (2001): 93–120.

of justification accepted by Lutherans remains decidedly forensic, with the insistence that the human person in not rendered inwardly purified from damnable sin. This is a fundamentally different perspective on the doctrine of justification than that held by Catholics, who see true human purity as the ultimate work of grace, and the source of the possibility of a real and authentic *merit* before God. For Catholics, justification must consist of something more than a mere *declaration* that salvation will be ours in spite of our wickedness; it must be a genuine renewal and elevation of the powers of the human person, such that we can be actively joined to God in a true, participatory friendship.

There can be no doubt that Christians have struggled to understand the mystery of human responsibility in light of God's omnipotence throughout our long history. The inherently difficult landscape of this mystery has been widely explored, and some tracts of it found to be more or less unforgiving than others—with some parts decidedly impassible. We find the path cut by (or at least *through*) Aquinas to be, for the most part, more direct and easily negotiated than the alternatives. It should be considered seriously by anyone truly interested in examining this mystery in good faith.

In the present work, we saw, therefore, that God causes human agency itself by exerting creative power over the human will, enabling it to act with respect to objects inherently beyond the scope of its natural power of operation. That elevation occurs as God undergirds the human will with an efficient causality *co-proximate* to that of the human will, but metaphysically *prior* to it. God's activity also involves a necessary dimension of *final causality*, whereby his self-presentation to the human person provides an *end* toward-which the human will can then choose to *move* by the new power provided by God *efficiently*. Some form of self-presentation by God is necessary for there to be any possibility of supra-natural movement on the part of the human being, because power or no power, there can be no *movement-toward* without a *definite direction*. In other words, there can be no *possibility-for* without a *possibility-making actuality*.

God is thus always the first cause of human agency, whether that causality is considered under the dimension of *efficiency* or *finality*. Still, the human person remains an agent in a real and meaningful sense, because while God relates the creature to himself as effect to cause, he does so in such a way as to cause the creature's power to act as an agent in its own right. This power, though itself caused, does not reduce to instrumentality, moreover, because God exercises agency over the creature *co-proximately.* He does not, in other words, merely *set the creature in motion,* but *engages* the creature's formal dimension of being, *facilitating the creature's own activity of choice.*

Because God's causal activity is *relationship-building,* the human being is made capable of *meriting* before God in a meaningful sense. The power of supra-natural agency is given, through the elevation of grace, by virtue of the indwelling of the Holy Spirit, fulfilling the *telos* of the human will—completing the ontological activity for which it was originally created. By so completing the ontological activity of the human will, the Holy Spirit relates to the will as if it were a kind of super-added form—that is, an activity-of-being over-and-above that natural to the substance in which it inheres, capable of elevating the *dignity* of that substance to the level of its own nobility. Thus, when a human being exercises the agency enabled by grace, that exercise has, not only the *power* of the enabler, but also the *dignity* of the enabler; and the human agent *merits* out of that *condignity.*

This merit is *real,* because the *exercise of agency* is that *proper to the human person;* but it remains *relative,* because it is only *made proper* through the super-addition of the divine presence in the human will. Indeed, it is not only *relative,* but *relational,* depending, for its very *esse,* upon God's *co-proximity* from-moment-to-moment. Though human beings can truly *merit* before God out of *condignity* with him, that power is wholly provided and sustained by God's power. According to this view, Pelagianism is untenable, because the human will can exercise no salvifically meaningful moral agency without grace. Likewise, because this thesis manages to *preserve* a truly meaningful sense of human agency, it avoids the pitfalls of radical Predestinarianism, and the counter-scriptural charge that God would create anyone for damnation (cf. 1 Tim 2:4). The present position, therefore, does more than simply avoid both Pelagianism and Predestinarianism. It provides a meaningful framework within which human beings can "work out their own salvation in fear and trembling" (cf. Phil 2:12b). Within this framework, Christians remain always aware of their dependency upon God, chastened by the reality of sin's consequences, and encouraged onward by the sure hope of salvation.

Bibliography

Aland, Barbara, et. al., eds. *The Greek New Testament*. Fouth Revised Edition. Stuttgart: Deutsche Bibelgesellshaft, United Bible Societies, 2003.

Anderson, H. George, et al., eds. *Justification by Faith* (Catholics and Lutherans in Dialogue: VII). Minneaplois: Augsburg Publishing House, 1985.

Aquinas, Saint Thomas. *Light of Faith: The Compendium of Theology*. Cyril Vollert, S.J., trans. Manchester, New Hampshire: Sophia Institute Press, 1993.

Aquinas, Saint Thomas. *Summa Contra Gentiles*, 5 vols. Anton C. Pagis, F.R.S.C., trans. Notre Dame: University of Notre Dame Press, 1975.

Aquinas St. Thomas. *Commentary on Aristotle's De Anima*. Kenelm Foster, O.P. and Silvester Humphries, O.P., trans. Notre Dame: Dumb Ox Books, 1994.

Aquinas, St. Thomas. *Commentary on Aristotle's Metaphysics*. John P. Rowan, trans. Notre Dame: Dumb Ox Books, 1995.

Aquinas, St. Thomas. *On Spiritual Creatures (De Spiritualibus Creaturis)*. Mary C. Fitzpatrick, Ph.D. and John J. Wellmuth, Ph.D., trans. (Mediaeval Philosophical Texts in Translation: 5). Milwaukee: Marquette University Press, 1949.

Aquinas, St Thomas. *Summa Theologiae*, vol. 31. T. C. O'Brien, trans. New York: McGraw-Hill Book Company, 1974.

Aquinas, St Thomas. *Summa Theologiae*, vol. 33. W. J. Hill, O.P., trans. New York: McGraw-Hill Book Company, 1966.

Aquinas, St Thomas. *Summa Theologiae*, vol. 34. R. J. Batten, O.P., trans. New York: McGraw-Hill Book Company, 1975.

Aquinas, St. Thomas. *Summa Theologica*, 3 vols. New York: Benzinger, 1947.

Aquinas, St. Thomas. *Truth*. Robert W. Mulligan, S.J., trans. Indianapolis: Hackett Publishing Company, Inc., 1994.

Aquinas, St. Thomas, O.P. *Questions on the Soul (Quaestiones de*

Anima). James H. Robb, trans. (Mediaeval Texts in Translation: 27). Milwaukee: Marquette University Press, 1984.

Aquinatis, S. Thomae. *Compendium Theologiae ad Fratrem Reginaldum Socium Suum Carissimum*. In, Aquinatis, S. Thomae. *Opuscula Theologica*, vol. 1. Taurini: Marietti, 1954. (13–138).

Aquinatis, S. Thomae. *In Metaphysicam Aristotelis Commentaria*. Taurini: Marietti, 1820.

Aquinatis, S. Thomae Doctoris Angelici. *Summa Theologiae*. Cum textu recensione Leonina. 4 vols. Romae: Marietti, 1948.

Aquino, Sancti Tomae de. *Quaestiones disputatae de veritate*. In Aquino, *Sancti Tomae de opera omnia* / jussu Leonis XIII P.M. edita; cura et studio Fratrum praedicatorum. Thomus XXII.

Aquino, Sancti Tomae de. *Summa Theologiae*. Alba: Editiones Paulinae, 1962.

Aristotle. *Categories*. J. A. Ackrill, trans. In, Barnes, Jonathan, ed. *The Complete Works of Aristotle*, vol. 1. (Bollingen Series LXXI: 2). Princeton University Press, 1984. (3–24).

Aristotle. *Metaphysics: Books Zeta, Eta, Theta, Iota (VII–X)*. Montgomery Furth, trans. Indianapolis: Hackett Publishing Company, 1985.

Aristotle. *Metaphysics*. W. D. Ross, trans. In, Barnes, Jonathan, ed. *The Complete Works of Aristotle*, vol. 2. (Bollingen Series LXXI: 2). Princeton: Princeton University Press, 1984. (1552–1728).

Aristotle. *Physics*. R. P. Hardie and R. K. Gaye, trans. In, Barnes, Jonathan, ed. *The Complete Works of Aristotle*, vol. 2. (Bollingen Series LXXI: 2). Princeton: Princeton University Press, 1984. (315–446).

Attwater, Donald. *The Dissident Eastern Churches*. Milwaukee: The Bruce Publishing Company, 1937.

Augsburg Confession, The. Reprinted from *The Book of Concord*. Muhlenberg Press, 1959.

Augustine, Saint. *On Free Choice of the Will*. Anna S. Benjamin and L. H. Hackstaff, trans. New York: MacMillan Library of Liberal Arts, 1989.

Augustine, Saint. *Sermons (148–183)*. In John E. Rotelle, O.S.A., ed. *The Works of Saint Augustine: A Translation for the 21st Century*. Pt. III, Vol. 5. Edmund Hill, O.P., trans. (New Rochelle, New York: New City Press, 1992.

Augustine, Saint. *The Spirit and the Letter*. In John E. Rotelle, O.S.A., ed. *The Works of Saint Augustine: A Translation for the 21st Century.* Pt. I, Vol. 23. Roland J. Teske, S.J., trans. (New Rochelle, New York: New City Press, 1997. (139-202).

Augustine, St. *On Continence [De Continentia].* Rev. C. L. Cornish, M.A. trans. In, Philip Shaff, D.D., LL.D., ed. *A Select Library of Nicene and Post-Nicene Fathers of the Christian Church.* Vol. III. New York: Charles Scribner's Sons, 1917. (377-393).

Augustine, St. *The Confessions of St. Augustine.* John K. Ryan, trans. New York: Doubleday, Image Books, 1960.

Augustine, St. *The Enchiridion; or On Faith, Hope, and Love.* Professor J. F. Shaw, trans. In, Philip Shaff, D.D., LL.D., ed. *A Select Library of Nicene and Post-Nicene Fathers of the Christian Church.* Vol. III. New York: Charles Scribner's Sons, 1917. (229-276).

Báñez, Domingo. *Comentarios Inéditos a la Prima Secundae de Santo Tomás,* 3 vols. Matriti, 1948.

Bloom, Allan. *The Closing of the American Mind.* New York: Simon and Schuster, 1987.

Bonaventure, St. *The Soul's Journey Into God (Itinerarium Mentis in Deum).* In, *Bonaventure.* (The Classics of Western Spirituality). Ewart Cousins, trans. New York: Paulist Press, 1978.

Bulzacchelli, Richard H. "Duns Scotus's Third 'Volitional Posture' and a Critique of the Problem of Moral Indifference in Our Time." *Franciscan Studies.* Vol. 58 (2000): 77-109.

Burleigh, John H., trans. *Augustine: Earlier Writings.* Philadelphia: The Westminster Press, 1953.

Brown, Raymond, S.S. *Priest and Bishop: Biblical Reflections.* New York: Paulist Press, 1970

Canons and Decrees of the Council of Trent. Rev. H. J. Scroeder, O.P., trans. Rockford, Illinois: TAN Books and Publishers, Inc., 1978.

Cassian, John. *The Conferences of John Cassian.* (Part I). Rev. Edgar C. S. Gibson, M.A., trans. In, Schaff, Philip, D.D., LL.D., and Henry Wace, D.D., eds. *A Select Library of Nicene and Post-Nicene Fathers of the Christian Church.* (Second Series). Vol. XI. New York: The Christian Literature Company, 1894. (291-545).

Cassian, John. *The Seven Books of John Cassian on the Incarnation of the Lord.* Rev. Edgar C. S. Gibson, M.A., trans. In, Schaff, Philip, D.D., LL.D., and Henry Wace, D.D., eds. *A Select Library of Nicene and Post-Nicene Fathers of the Christian Church.* (Second Series). Vol. XI. New York: The Christian Literature Company, 1894. (457-

621).

Catechism of the Catholic Church. 2nd ed. Washington, D.C.: United States Catholic Conference, 2000.

Catechism of the Council of Trent for Parish Priests. John A. McHugh, O.P., S.T.M., Litt.D. and Charles J. Callan, O.P., S.T.M., Litt.D., trans. Rockford, Illinois, TAN Books and Publishers, Inc., 1982.

Clarke, W. Norris, S.J. *Person and Being.* (The Aquinas Lecture, 1993). Milwaukee: Marquette University Press, 1993.

Cognet, L. J. "Jansenism." In, *The New Catholic Encyclopedia.* Vol. VII. Washington, DC: Catholic University of America, 1967. (820–824).

De Intellectu *Attributed to Alexander of Aphrodesias, The.* In, Schroeder, Frederic M. and Robert B. Todd, trans. *Two Greek Aristotelian Commentators on the Intellect.* (Medieval Sources in Translation: 33). Toronto: Pontifical Institute of Medieval Studies, 1990.

Delumeau, Jean. *Catholicism between Luther and Voltaire: A New View of the Counter Reformation.* Westminster: John Knox Press, 1977.

Denzinger, Henry. *The Sources of Christian Dogma.* Roy J. Deferrari, trans. (from *Enchiridion Symbolorum.* 30th ed.). Binghamton, NY: B. Herder Book Co. 1957.

Eusebius. *The Church History of Eusebius.* Rev. Arthur Cushman McGiffert, Ph.D., trans. In, Schaff, Philip, D.D., LL.D., and Henry Wace, D.D., eds. *A Select Library of Nicene and Post-Nicene Fathers of the Christian Church* (Second Series). Vol. I. New York: The Christian Literature Company, 1890. (1–403).

Farrelly, Dom M. John, O.S.B. *Predestination, Grace, and Free Will.* Westminster, Maryland: The Newman Press, 1964.

Flannery, Austin, O.P., ed. *The Conciliar and Post Conciliar Documents.* (Vatican Council II: vol. 1). Northport, New York: Costello Publishing Company, Inc., 1996.

Fritschel, George J. *The Formula of Concord: Its Origins and Contents.* Philadelphia, Pennsylvania: The Lutheran Publication Society, 1916.

Gruber, Mark, O.S.B. *Journey Back to Eden: My Life and Times among the Desert Fathers.* M. Michele Ransil, C.D.P., ed. Maryknoll, New York: Orbis Books, 2002.

Gruber, Mark, O.S.B. *Sacrifice in the Desert: A Study of an Egyptian*

Minority Through the Prism of Coptic Monasticism. M. Michele Ransil, C.D.P., ed. Lanham, MD: University Press of America, 2003.

Hennessey, Justin, O.P. *Grace*. 3rd ed. Emmitsburg, Maryland: Mt. St. Mary Seminary Press, 1988.

Hill, W. J. "Báñez and Bañezianism." *The New Catholic Encyclopedia*. Vol. II. Washington, DC: Catholic University of America, 1967. (48–50).

John Paul II. *The Mercy of God: Dives in Misericordia*. 30 November, 1980. Vatican translation. Boston: St. Paul Books & Media, 1980.

John Paul II. *Fides et Ratio: On the Relationship between Faith and Reason*. September 14, 1998. Vatican translation. Boston: Pauline Books & Media,1998.

"Joint Declaration on the Doctrine of Justification." *Origins*. Vol. 28:8 (1998): 120–121.

Lewis, C. S. *Mere Christianity*. Revised and Enlarged Edition. New York: Macmillan Publishing Co., 1952.

Macrae, G. W. "Mandaean Religion." *New Catholic Encyclopedia*. Vol, IX. Washington, DC: Catholic University of America, 1967. (145).

Malloy, Christopher J. "The Nature of Justifying Grace: A Lacuna in the *Joint Declaration*." *The Thomist*. Vol. 65 (2001): 93–120.

McNiell, ed. *Calvin: Institutes of the Christian Religion*, F. L. Battles, trans. 2 vols. Philadelphia: Westminster Press, 1960.

Molina D. Ludovico. *Concordia Liberi Arbitrii cum Gratiae Donis, Divina Præscientia, Providentia, Prædestinatione, et Reprobatione*. Sumptibus et Typis P. Lethielleux, Editoris. Parisiis, 1876.

Neuhaus, Richard John. *The Catholic Moment: The Paradox of the Church in the Modern World*. San Francisco: Harper & Row, Publishers, 1987.

Nietzsche, Friedrich. *The Gay Science*. Walter Kaufmann, trans. New York: Vantage Books, 1974.

O'Connor, W. R. "Molina and Bañez as Interpreters of Aquinas." *New Scholasticism*. vol 21 (1947): 243–259.

Plato. *Protagoras*. W. K. C. Guthrie, trans. In, Hamilton, Edith and Huntington Cairns, eds. *Plato: The Collected Dialogues*. (Bollingen Series LXXI). Princeton: Princeton University Press, 1961. (747–772).

Ratzinger, Joseph Cardinal. *Introduction to Christianity*. J. R. Foster, trans. San Francisco: Communio Books/Ignatius Press, 1990.

Ratzinger, Joseph. *The Theology of History in St. Bonaventure.* Zachary Hayes, O.F.M., trans. Chicago: Chicago University Press, 1971.

Rayan, T. "Congregatio De Auxiliis." *The New Catholic Encyclopedia.* Vol. IV. Washington, DC: Catholic University of America, 1967. (168–171).

Ries, J. "Manichaeism." *New Catholic Encyclopedia.* Vol, IX. Washington, DC: Catholic University of America, 1967. (153–160).

Second Helvetic Confession. In, *The Constitution of the United Presbyterian Church of the United States of America, Part I: Book of Confessions.* New York: The General Assembly of the United Presbyterian Church of the United States of America, 1967. (5.001–5.260).

Senior, Donald, et al., eds. *The Catholic Study Bible.* The New American Bible Translation. New York: Oxford University Press, 1990.

Smith, Jonathan Z., et al., eds. *The HarperCollins Dictionary of Religion.* New York: HarperSanFrancisco, 1995.

Westminster Confession of Faith. In, *The Constitution of the United Presbyterian Church of the United States of America, Part I: Book of Confessions.* New York: The General Assembly of the United Presbyterian Church of the United States of America, 1967. (6.001–6.178).

About the Author

Richard H. Bulzacchelli took the B.A. in philosophy at Saint Vincent College in Latrobe, Pennsylvania, the M.A. in Christian philosophy at Marquette University, the M.A. in religious studies at Providence College, and the S.T.L. in systematic theology from the Pontifical Faculty of the Immaculate Conception at the Dominican House of Studies in Washington, DC. He is currently working on a dissertation for the S.T.D. at the International Marian Research Institute in Dayton, Ohio.

Apart from his work in the present volume, Mr. Bulzacchelli has spoken and written professionally on the question of human freedom, most notably in, "Duns Scotus's Third 'Volitional Posture' and a Critique of the Problem of Moral Indifference in Our Time," *Franciscan Studies* (vol. 58, 2000: 77–109). Mr. Bulzacchelli taught philosophy at Saint Francis University in Loretto, Pennsylvania, before accepting his present position at Aquinas College in Nashville, Tennessee, where he teaches theology. He lives in Nashville with his wife, Kay, and his three children, Brea, Athanasius, and Faustina.

www.ingramcontent.com/pod-product-compliance
Lightning Source LLC
Chambersburg PA
CBHW021130300426
44113CB00006B/361